DO **MORE** GOOD

MOVING NONPROFITS FROM
GOOD TO GROWTH

BILL MCKENDRY

WITH KATHLEEN SINDORF

Forefront
BOOKS

Dedication

This book is dedicated to my Lord, wife, sons, family, friends, and cohorts. They all have inspired me to always strive to do more good.

Also, a special callout to my parents—John and Lois McKendry. They showed me that disabilities are only handicaps if you allow them to be. And they inspired me to be a voice for those who need help.

Table of Contents

PART III
DIRECTION

PART IV
EXPRESSION

PART V

ACTION

PART VI

SUCCESS

Foreword

I've been given a lot of business books—I mean, *a lot* of business books.

When you've been in the business and marketing world as long as I have, you work alongside many astute business minds. And it would seem they are all published and each has insights to share.

Many have original concepts to consider or catchy phrases to memorize. But I would argue that few books are as comprehensive as *Do More Good*. Soup to nuts, as they say, Bill has seen it, done it, and can write authoritatively about it. From asking hard questions to providing clear answers, Bill identifies what makes a nonprofit organization a unique animal and how a purposeful and best-practices approach works best when innovating. He not only provides a roadmap toward realizing what success looks like, he tells you how to recognize it when you get there. His IDEAS Process helps keep "the main thing the main thing," as Stephen Covey so aptly said.

Bill and I first met in Grand Rapids, Michigan, in the early 2000s when I spoke at an event held at Cornerstone University. I was in C-level leadership in the corporate world then (Domino's Pizza), and Bill had already made the transition from the for-profit to the nonprofit world. I quickly recognized his heart for service as well as his willingness to step out of the comfortable and into the meaningful. It was inspiring. With years of varied experience in the for-profit and nonprofit space, Bill comes to you as an award-winning and seasoned marketer. *Do More Good* truly speaks to his heart and passions.

I believe that it's a privilege to work with others who see "need" as not just an academic exercise, but as a call for change. There are deeper truths to be realized in trying to reach the hearts of others. The best innovation, the kind that breaks through and breaks into our overly digitalized and fractured world, has to be based on these truths. Bill not only understands this, he lives and promotes it. I would argue there isn't anyone who comes to this topic so well prepared and with so much personal experience. He doesn't merely react to the cultural zeitgeist—he *is* and has been on the leading edge of real cultural response and change for years. I guess you could say he was doing good before doing good was cool.

I am honored to be included in his book, and I appreciate the opportunity to speak to my own experiences making the transition from the corporate space to the not-for-profit world. I never could have imagined the learning, the challenges, and the rewards that awaited me. I made the move to Compassion International in 2017, and in the span of these four years, the world has changed profoundly in so many ways. But I am grateful to be used by God to serve in this way, putting my own stamp on the ideas and practices of doing more good.

Martin Luther King Jr. famously said, "The time is always right to do what is right." I couldn't agree more. The times we live in cry out for a compassionate approach to growth and innovation. Change is inevitable. But meaningful and purposeful innovation can make change something to embrace, not to fear, something to lead people toward, not drag people into.

I congratulate Bill on writing such an important book. My wife is a writer, and I have seen how consuming and laborious the writing process can be. Writers pore over every word, phrase, and idea. And they personally put a lot of themselves into each process and project. I'm not sure I always understood that. I appreciate it all the more now.

My hope is that you appreciate the heart and effort that went into this book, and that you are encouraged by the stories within and inspired to "do more good," however that looks for you.

Ken Calwell
Chief Marketing Officer, SVP Innovation
Compassion International
Colorado Springs, Colorado

How Bad Do You Want to Do Good?

Jimmy Smith is a highly accomplished advertising and marketing pro. As an African-American from a blue-collar community in Michigan, he's had to work really hard and overcome a lot of obstacles to get to where he is today, which is working for the biggest and best-known brands and advertising agencies in the world.

When I invited him to speak at the first national conference for our nonprofit organization DO MORE GOOD, and then asked him if he'd do so for free, it seemed like a longshot. But truth be told, I did have a slight personal connection with Jimmy, so it was worth a try. We had been high school classmates, and though we'd never become close friends, I knew who he was and I had been following his career for several decades. So when we spoke (for the first time in thirty-nine years) and I asked him to be our keynote speaker for this inaugural conference, Jimmy was open about his desire to help, and I was open about being one of his biggest fans.

Jimmy's presentation title was "How Big Is Your WHY?" (an inspiring topic I'll cover later in this book). While I thought that sounded like great content to close our first-ever national conference, his speech, refreshingly, wasn't a checklist of dos and don'ts about powerful storytelling and branding. Rather, it was about his personal journey to do good work, his passion to use his gifts to make lasting change and to do *more* good. His inspiring life story included many heartbreaking experiences of persecution and racism, but he never lost his desire to do more than just make a living with his talents. Those horrible things he endured fueled an inner burning passion to courageously pursue every opportunity to make a difference.

Jimmy ended his speech with a total "mic drop" moment when he asked our conference crowd of nonprofit executives, leaders, and communicators this profound question: "How bad do you want to do good?"

I've been challenged by that statement ever since.

That's the purpose of this book—like Jimmy, I feel called to do more good with my talent and expertise. And I want to do good . . . really, really bad.

I've learned I can do this by combining my background and experiences in marketing and branding for some of the world's biggest brands such as American Express, Target, Dodge, Kohler, and Taco Bell, and that I can use this knowledge and insights to help nonprofits compete better for people's discretionary time and money.

I've also created several tools and concepts that can be uniquely deployed by nonprofits to help them generate more awareness and support. By following these methods, nonprofits will be armed with proven practices and processes to increase their returns and impact.

This book is structured in a way that it is both a blueprint to build and a roadmap to follow. In the first eight chapters, I outline some foundational concepts that nonprofits must understand and grasp to be more successful to gain the attention and support they need to grow audience consideration and their organizational resources.

Once this blueprint has been established, I then provide a roadmap to develop a stronger brand, which is pivotal to the success of any institution or organization. Throughout most of this book you will be guided through my proprietary **IDEAS** process where you'll learn to start with **(I)**nsights to develop a **(D)**irection and formulate a stronger brand (E)xpression. This will lead you to taking new (A)ction in the market and using a variety of solid metrics to measure (S)uccess.

In each step of the **IDEAS** process overview, I will provide you with specific ways to analyze, create, and refine your brand and marketing efforts to develop breakthrough program elements and maximize success.

It's taken me over thirty years in the marketing business and experience consulting with more than 300 nonprofit organizations to pull this book together. It's not even in my best interest to share most of this with you in the detail I have. After all, I should just be using this information to grow my business and my client base. But it has been laid on my heart that this information is too important not to share.

So do you want to do good as bad as Jimmy and I do? Then please . . . do read, do understand, do follow, do challenge, do share, do create, do inform, do push, do forward, do whatever it takes to do *more* good.

~Bill McKendry

PART I

GETTING ON THE SAME PAGE

CHAPTER 1

Homeless for a Day

Being a creative person at heart, I've worked with many renowned brands over my extended career in marketing, advertising, and communications. Some of them are surprised to learn that research and discovery are the first things I do when beginning work for any new client or initiative. One reason why I begin with these is because I earned my advertising degree through the business school of my college while also majoring in marketing. Most creative people in our industry get an advertising degree through the school of communication. As a result, they miss studying and understanding the strategic underpinnings that drive breakthrough communication and generate superior outcomes. What I've learned is to be disciplined about doing primary and/or secondary research before formulating *any* initial recommendations—even when immediate needs and solutions may seem like no-brainers.

In working with typical business clients, "discovery" can include a plant tour, working for a day with salespeople to understand how products and services are sold, or meeting with top executives to discuss their business model and vision for achieving success.

But for my first client in the nonprofit sector, a struggling 95-year-old homeless shelter, it meant living as a homeless person for a day, including spending a night sleeping on a cot at the mission. For full disclosure, I must admit this was my business partner's idea and not mine! But it turned out to be one of the best and most memorable things I've ever done to get to know a client's business and its impact on the people it serves.

After just one night at the rescue mission, my perceptions of what causes someone to be in a homeless situation dramatically changed. Frankly, I had often wondered how someone could possibly allow themselves to end up homeless. I used to wonder if it was because homeless people were lazy or simply preferred to drink and do drugs instead of working like normal people. I wrongly believed the homeless were responsible for putting themselves on the street by not being motivated enough to get a job and conform to the norms of society.

After that night at the mission, though, I was set straight forever. I discovered that homeless people don't choose to be homeless; they're victims of their circumstances. Maybe they lost a spouse, child, or family member. Maybe they served in the armed forces and were traumatized by what they experienced. Perhaps they grew up in a family of substance abusers or suffered through emotional, physical, or sexual abuse as a child. Maybe they are mentally ill and cannot afford treatment.

On that one, hot August night at the rescue mission I learned that homeless people likely suffer from not just one, but many of these life-altering issues—some of the people staying at this rescue mission I talked to seemed to suffer from *all* of them!

I also learned that homeless people often feel like they are drowning in circumstances beyond their control. They've burned through their support system or had no support system to help them—maybe even as a child.

I didn't just learn about the *causes* of homelessness; I experienced the *results* of homelessness for the first time in my life. And that tiny, ridiculously small taste of it changed my perspective forever.

Ultimately we created a few campaigns that helped the rescue mission and the people it serves. I've helped many other rescue missions and people in homeless situations since then, though they've helped me a lot more than I've ever helped them. That one visit gave me insights and understanding that I could help other nonprofit organizations with my skills and expertise. In fact, it changed the trajectory of my entire career.

Long before there was success, there was the storyboard.

After my day of homelessness, I felt I had the insights needed to create an impactful ad campaign that would help bring the rescue mission greater awareness and support. My team determined that a television commercial would be the key element to launch the campaign. Before we could create a television ad, we first had to develop a storyboard as a tool to visually communicate the concept to our client.

Our concept was ambitious: The entire spot was to be filmed underwater. My partner assured me we could pull this off. He even promised to build the set we needed—an urban alley scene—in his garage. To top it off, we found a condo complex with an indoor pool that was willing to allow us to sink our set in their water-filled pool and give us a few days to shoot the spot.

We were nervous, but it wasn't just the magnitude of the TV spot's production that worried us. Even though my business partner and I had pitched thousands of campaigns to business clients, the pressure of doing something for an organization in such great need was more daunting than anything we had previously done. This wasn't just about selling products—it was about changing lives!

Before we could begin our storyboard presentation, the mission's executive director asked if we could pray. That was just the first thing that made this a different presentation from all the others in our corporate agency life. In fact, once the session was finished, I'll never forget the executive director's reaction to our work.

Then the pitch.

We presented the storyboard just as we had done for many for-profit companies in the past. We walked through the visual concept, explaining what would happen in the television ad, frame by frame.

My partner, the art and film director, explained the storyboard with great precision. He walked through how the spot would begin in an alley with just one homeless woman. Then three homeless men would drift into the alley from above, bubbles coming out of their mouths. At that point, the viewer realizes that the entire alley scene, and everyone in it, is underwater. My partner stopped short of revealing the final scene, covering the final frame on the storyboard with his hand. The executive director and his development director were on the edges of their seats.

Just before the last frame was revealed, it was my turn. As the writer, I read the narration copy: "The average American family is three paychecks away from being homeless." My partner noted that those words would appear over the scene.

I continued reading: "Add to that substance abuse, mental illness, and the death of a spouse or family member . . ." My partner explained that those words would also appear over the imagery as more homeless men dropped into the scene.

I continued: ". . . and soon, you can find yourself in pretty deep water. At Mel Trotter Ministries, we not only help homeless people with food and shelter . . ."

My partner then revealed the last frame, explaining that at this point in the spot, a hand would come into the scene from above and pull one of the homeless men up to the surface and out of the alley.

I finished the script by reading the closing line: ". . . we help them find a way out."

And then, the reaction we never expected (and will never forget).

The executive director looked at us, his eyes welling up with tears, and then he put his head down on the conference table. It was obvious he was trying to compose himself, but my partner and I did not fully understand why. We exchanged a few glances with the development director, and she seemed as confused as we were.

Once the executive director composed himself, he said, "Guys, I'm reacting this way for two reasons. The first is that you just showed me the power of a parable. Like Jesus did, you used a very compelling story to make a very powerful point. I've seen others do it—pastors, fundraisers, teachers—but I never expected it to come from a TV commercial . . . and from a couple of advertising guys."

Then he said, "Come with me. I want to show you the other reason I reacted so emotionally." The executive director led us outside to the back of the mission and pointed to a huge trash container. This was no ordinary dumpster; this was the kind you see at large construction sites. He then informed us that the container was one of the biggest monthly expenses for the struggling mission.

He asked us, "Do you know why we have to have a dumpster that large?"

We had no idea. He said, "We need it just to dispose of so many of the donations that get dropped off here." He went on, "You see, people come here every day and give us their garbage. Clothes that are worn out, items that are broken, and things that are no longer useful. They convince themselves that they're giving us a donation, but they're just dropping off their trash. You guys, you guys [he composed himself again] . . . did not bring us your garbage. You brought us your *best* work. Thank you. *Thank you!*"

When good is not good enough.

I'll never forget that day or that message. They have inspired me to want to do more good, but more importantly, to make sure I always do my absolute best when working with nonprofit clients.

Corporate clients, because they have big budgets, well-trained staff, and great research, just naturally demand the best out of you. However, sometimes it's easy to let up and say, "This will do," when you're working with a nonprofit that has a tight budget and fewer resources. But frankly, "good enough" is just not sufficient when it comes to dealing with nonprofits that don't have enough resources to do all the good that is needed.

Chances are, if you're reading this book, you have a personal mission to do more good. And frankly, that's a great calling.

Martin Luther King Jr. once gave a speech about how important it is to do the good work we're called to do with uncompromising excellence. The famous excerpt is:

> "Now the thing about the length of life: after accepting ourselves and our tools, we must discover what we are called to do. And once we discover it, we should set out to do it with all of the strength and all of the power that we have in our systems. And after we've discovered what God called us to do, after we've discovered our life's work, we should set out to do that work so well that the living, the dead, or the unborn couldn't do it any better ... What I'm saying to you this morning, my friends, even if it falls on your lot to be a street sweeper, go on out and sweep streets like Michelangelo painted pictures; sweep streets like Handel and Beethoven composed music; sweep streets like Shakespeare wrote poetry; sweep streets so well that all the host of heaven and earth will have to pause and say, 'Here lived a great street sweeper who swept his job well.'"[1]

I feel this same calling to do more good. In the process of using my gifts to help, I've learned the greatest satisfaction and results come not just from doing good ... but by doing good to the greatest capacity I can.

If we're working to the best of our abilities to understand and communicate with the people we serve, then we won't be trying to grab the glory for ourselves or create a campaign just to get noticed or win awards. Part of doing *more* good means being willing to listen and respond, even if no one notices your good work. Approach your "discovery" phase with an open mind and prepare to be amazed at what you learn!

CHAPTER 2

Moving from Doing Good to Doing *More* Good

Imagine for a moment that you're at a critical point in your life.

You're jobless and your savings account is dwindling fast. Your wife needs you to find employment because you've got children to clothe and feed. To make matters worse, several elderly family members have come to live with you and are counting on you for support. And because of circumstances beyond their control, no one in your family is able to work—except for you.

Now imagine that your first response to this situation is to look for a new car to carry your bigger family. Then you begin looking for a larger home so everyone can live more comfortably. You also believe you need to hire a housekeeper to help your wife. Then you meet with an accountant to discuss your shrinking financial resources and work out a budget to help you carefully manage your remaining cash.

While all this is happening, you meet regularly with life coaches, friends, and consultants who counsel you on your priorities (but curiously, not on finding a job). You then have this sudden inspiration—you could throw a huge dinner party and invite friends and business owners to network with you, hoping someone will offer you a solution! During the gathering, you openly discuss your financial needs…but *not* the fact that you're unemployed!

Deep down, you know that getting a job should be your highest priority, yet you haven't even begun working on a resume. You haven't filled out an application or done any online networking. You haven't researched the job market. Even at the most basic level, you haven't thought about, much less considered, how to articulate with any clarity what differentiates you from others looking for work.

Who would do something like this?

Unfortunately, this is exactly how many nonprofit organizations manage their marketing and branding efforts. They ignore them or, at best, put them on the back burner and hope the need for donors and volunteers will solve itself. Instead of putting time and thought into marketing, they form advisory boards, seek financial and legal counsel, manage and improve facilities, and even put together huge, expensive, and inefficient fundraisers in the hopes that all their financial problems will be magically solved.

Why Does This Happen?

For starters, spending money on marketing and branding isn't exactly encouraged by the nonprofit community. Many charity-rating services frown upon dollars used for marketing, and they lower their approval scores accordingly. Some donors and board members see marketing efforts as an unnecessary expense for nonprofit organizations (though these same donors and board members likely have first-hand knowledge that branding and marketing play essential roles in the success of their own for-profit businesses).

Beyond that, most nonprofits see themselves as needs-driven organizations. Therefore, every dollar that doesn't go to a need or population they're serving is seen as a dollar diverted from doing good work.

What's the Solution?

My work with nonprofits is all about changing that perspective. It's about getting nonprofits to see marketing and branding as an investment—not an expense. It's also about making fundraising more effective and efficient. And it's about being more responsible, proactive, and wise in getting people to respond to your organization's needs.

This journey to change perspectives and practices began long before there was a DO MORE GOOD movement or nonprofit organization. It began when I helped to start an advertising/marketing agency named Hanon McKendry. This agency's vision and mission inspired much of what I do today.

Hanon McKendry began as a start-up firm in a small-but-growing city in the Midwest. My business partner, Jim Hanon, and I were at turning points in our careers. We had both worked at large, multinational agencies in much bigger towns and had built successful reputations, but we were left wondering if our occupations aligned with our vocations. In other words, were we just working for a living or doing what we were really destined and "called" to do?

While we loved being able to use our abilities to communicate artfully and persuasively, we were feeling unsatisfied and empty using our talents only to sell things that encouraged materialism in consumers. Jim and I had known each other for years and were both men of faith, but we each had the unsettling feeling that something was still missing, and that perhaps there was something more we were supposed to do with our lives.

One day during a lunch meeting, I asked Jim, "Did God create us to sell credit cards, burgers, tacos, and home-improvement merchandise . . . or does He want our talents to be used for other things instead?"

Jim said, "Hmmm . . . that's interesting. Let me ask you this: What kind of agency do you think Jesus would want us to be part of?"

These two questions turned that lunch meeting into a discussion that stretched into dinner and then into an ideation session that lasted until the wee hours of the next morning.

A voice to advocate for those who need help.

We determined that Jesus would want us to be a purpose-driven voice for struggling people and causes that need help. He'd want us working at a firm where we could be a counterbalance to the selfish, materialistic world . . . to be an agent for charity, faith, hope, and human kindness.

The tagline we created for this breakthrough agency was: "Really good advertising for really good things." If the Hanon McKendry agency were started in 2021, it would fit right in with the trend of businesses mixing their purpose and doing good to attract today's more cause-concerned consumers. But that wasn't our motivation, nor was it the market environment we were facing then. Frankly, in 1994, our new agency was seen by many of our peers and the business community as somewhat utopian and impractical.

Fortunately, we had a few clients who believed in us and a pack of employees who also wanted to make a difference—not just a living—and together we set out to do more good.

Because of that spirit and willingness to risk ridicule, revenue, and even careers in the pursuit of good, I believe that we have been given the grace to be part of many impactful opportunities that have gone well beyond our influence or control.

Be careful what you ask for.

One of those moments came in 1996 when we had the opportunity to film Mother Teresa, a year before her death. This came about, quite literally, as the result of a joke during a client meeting.

Our client was interested in creating short films and commercials to make a difference by influencing the perspectives of Catholic women. We were sitting at the table with several people, discussing possible approaches with the client, when I made a side comment to my business partner. I jokingly said under my breath, "Maybe we should get Mother Teresa as a spokesperson!" I was just being goofy to lighten the mood.

Somebody overheard me and asked, "What did you say, Bill?"

"Nothing," I said. "I was just joking around with my colleague, Jim."

Jim said, "Bill thinks we should get Mother Teresa as a spokes-person. Ha, ha, ha..."

And the client asked, "Are you serious about that?"

I said, "Well, about serious as I could possibly be. Because we have no connections to Mother Teresa. So, no..."

The client then went on to say, "Well, she's coming to the United States in a few weeks to celebrate forty years of her work in Calcutta. She's being honored with a dinner at the White House. So if you're serious about wanting to film her, we can make that happen."

And so our client set it up for us to film Mother Teresa!

Peter Drucker has nothing on this sister.

We found ourselves in Washington, D.C., standing outside a convent where Mother Teresa was staying for her engagement at the White House. The video crew, my business partner, and I were going through the normal preproduction protocols. One standard practice is to get a signed model release before filming.

While it seemed crazy to ask Mother Teresa to sign a model release, to legally protect everyone involved, it just needed to be done. Representing Mother Teresa was a younger nun, Sister Sylvia, who was acting as her handler.

Mother Teresa was eighty-six years old at the time, so Sister Sylvia was, my guess, about seventy-two years old. She and I reviewed the contents of the model release and other documents that needed to be signed to get our paperwork in order.

During our discussion, Sister Sylvia asked me to explain what I did, what Hanon McKendry was about, and how we worked for our clients. In a nutshell, I explained that we helped our clients, over 50 percent of which were nonprofits, to communicate more powerfully and persuasively—which then would help them raise the support they need so they don't just do good—they can do *even greater* good.

I said, "Maybe you know, Peter Drucker says a nonprofit organization's purpose isn't just the cause it's working for, but even more, its purpose is to raise the donors and funds needed to make the impact they are hoping to make. And like the business world, it takes resources to grow your impact, so communications and marketing provide the fuel needed to grow."

At this point, I was sure I had lost this sprightly seventy-two-year-old nun with my diatribe. Instead she looked at me and said, "I get it, Bill."

I responded, "Sister, I mean no disrespect, but I know a lot of really smart nonprofit CEOs who don't get what I just said. Can you tell me, in your own words, your understanding of this concept? We're a relatively new firm, and I'd love to know what I have said that might have resonated with you."

She said, "Mother Teresa and I talk about this topic all the time. We use a different wording to describe our needed focus on getting support, and it's this: 'No margin, no mission.'"

She then went on to say, "Do you think Mother Teresa really wanted to come to America and speak at the White House? No, not really. She would prefer to be back in Calcutta, helping people. Do you think she really wants the attention that goes with accepting awards like the Nobel Peace Prize? No, she doesn't seek any attention. She wants to stay in Calcutta and give her attention to the people there. But the reason she gets on a plane, comes to Washington, D.C., or goes to accept the Nobel Peace Prize in Sweden, the reason she does all this stuff at the age of eighty-six is because she understands, 'No margin, no mission.' If we don't raise money and awareness, we can't help the people we really want to help."

No margin, no mission.

That statement "No margin, no mission" stuck with me, and it's forever impacted the way I look at nonprofit organization marketing. Mother Teresa got it. And so did Sister Sylvia.

They understood why communicating your needs powerfully is so vitally important. If the Missionaries of Charity (the nonprofit Mother Teresa founded) didn't have the public awareness and financial support it needs, it wouldn't be able to continue its amazing work. It wasn't Mother Teresa's desire to be filmed or attend a fancy dinner in her honor. She much preferred to put on her sandals and serve the poor and sick and abandoned people of India, but she was wise enough to realize that she couldn't continue to do that good work—as famous and admired as she already was—if she didn't find ways to tell people about it! She wanted to do *more* good! And did she ever!

On the flight home from Washington, D.C., reflecting on all that transpired and feeling exhausted, I panicked for a moment and wondered if I'd remembered to get a copy of the model release with Mother Teresa's signature. I dug hastily through my backpack and pulled out the model release. It read at the bottom, "God bless you" and her signature, "Mother Teresa."

I don't like to display many pieces of work I've helped to create over the years, partly because I'm critical of myself and believe I can always do better. But that model release is still displayed in my agency today. My purpose for doing so isn't to showcase what I've done. Rather, I use it to remind and inspire myself and others what can be done when you believe strongly in the power and desire to do good.

CHAPTER 3

You Can Add
or Multiply

Some nonprofits substitute the word "fundraising" when they speak of their marketing efforts. Many more nonprofits put all their marketing resources toward fundraising, and that practice, oddly enough, is limiting their ability to raise funds.

I say that because, at their core, fundraising tactics rely heavily on one-to-one personal selling. Marketing, on the other hand, is about one organization selling to many. Which means, fundraising is like addition while marketing is like multiplication.

They both have a goal to raise funds—and they're both important. Yet marketing and fundraising are very different.

What Leads to Exponential Growth?

Most new and small nonprofit organizations have limited funds, so they naturally gravitate toward fundraising and development professionals as a way to create donor interest and bring in immediate dollars. While the initial investment may seem smaller than initiating a marketing program, many nonprofits fail to realize that there are significant uncalculated costs to deploying a development team, especially when it's the only method that's used.

The unanticipated cost of replicating and growing these efforts often includes hiring additional, experienced personnel. Because development is a very labor-intensive and highly skilled profession, nonprofits often need to add higher paid, more experienced development staff to grow the program. A development officer, or even a fundraising event, can only reach a limited number of people.

In short, development is about chasing a particular group of donors and asking them for gifts, while marketing is about creating considerable interest among broader audiences and giving everyone reasons to give.

Marketing Divides and Eventually Subtracts

A core marketing strategy is to segment (divide) and prioritize potential donors to maximize efforts and create compelling messages that connect with many different donors on many different levels. By doing this, an organization creates multiple revenue streams from a larger pool of donors.

Contrast that with development officers who only have so much time and as a result, tend to stay focused on larger gifts and wealthier individuals—a critically important, but very limited, crowd.

Plus, a primary objective of any truly successful marketing program is to decrease the cost of selling. The initial investments in a good marketing program have a return on investment (ROI) that continues to grow, and costs that continue to shrink over time. Let's see how the math works!

You Need an Air Attack to Go with Your Ground Game

I'm not saying that organizations shouldn't use or hire development professionals. Of course, most nonprofit organizations *need* strong advancement officers and should do all they can to support them.

Coming from the corporate branding world perspective, the marketing structure nearly always includes a vice president of marketing and a vice president of sales. And they are known to be separate functions with their own roles and responsibilities.

When I came into the nonprofit world, there were usually only titles such as "director of development" or "advancement officer." In reality, all these titles essentially equate to some level of "personal selling." In other words, this is really the sales force for a nonprofit.

Curiously, though, I've come across very few nonprofit organizations with a "vice president of marketing."

When I'm asked to make a presentation to a nonprofit or its board of directors, it's usually pretty obvious that I'm covering topics related to marketing and advertising. Yet during the introductions, I am often labeled as a "media guy," or a "public relations guy," or maybe a "communications guy."

It's as if words such as "marketing," "branding," and "advertising" are dirty, profit-focused words to be avoided in the nonprofit landscape.

The reality is, as in the corporate world, marketing and fundraising (personal selling) need to be a team—they are both responsible for maximizing potential and generating revenue for a nonprofit. But they can't and don't work well independently of each other.

A simple analogy I use to show how marketing and fundraising teams need to work together is to think of marketing as the "air attack" and fundraising as the "ground troops."

When you're going into the battleground of the marketplace, being prepared for the war for awareness demands an "air attack" that goes ahead of the ground troops to prepare the way. It softens the ground . . . it clears the trees . . . it lets people know that you're coming.

You might say that an air attack creates the environment for success for the ground troops to come in and do their work. It takes care of the "top of the funnel" work so that a fundraiser doesn't need to also carry the burden for making the organization known to its contacts. Instead, they can focus their efforts on what fundraisers are good at: developing relationships that create strong bonds with an organization, resulting in financial gifts.

If your organization does marketing right, the ground forces can come in and say to a donor, "You've obviously already seen or heard about the good that this organization does . . . now what kind of impact do you want to help us make?"

If you try to lead all donors through the sales funnel exclusively via fundraising, that's the equivalent of a general trying to win a war with only a ground attack. Modern generals would never do that! That would be like using Civil War tactics in which soldiers were expected to win exclusively through man-to-man combat and walking up to people to stab them. Deploying a ground attack strategy exclusively is not only brutal and outdated, it's also very inefficient—both in warfare and in revenue growth!

A few years ago, I told an audience at Cause Camp this analogy about the need for both "air attacks" and "ground troops," and it made enough of an impact that *Forbes* magazine reported it in the article, "Twitter's Top Four Nonprofit Takeaways From Cause Camp."[2]

This concept, I've been told, sheds light on what many leaders within nonprofit organizations instinctively know, but often struggle to communicate to their boards—that the old ways of expecting the development team to create awareness *and* build/advance relationships just aren't as effective as they once were. Certainly in this pandemic-impacted world, donors desire fewer in-person meetings, which makes using other methods to connect and communicate with your supporters a "must-have" going forward versus a "nice-to-have."

Here are some of the distinctions between fundraising and marketing to clarify the orientations of each discipline:

FUNDRAISING ORIENTATION	MARKETING ORIENTATION
Emphasis is on the individual	Emphasis is on the market
Adds donors through one-to-one or limited-reach efforts	Multiplies donor opportunities through one-to-many efforts
Focus is on organizational needs	Focus is on donor desires, needs, and wants
Management is sales-volume driven	Management drives growth through reach and frequency
Short-term for today's needs	Long-term planning for immediate needs and future goals
Views donor as the last link in organizational success	Views donor creation as the primary purpose of the organization
Fundraising is marketing	Marketing includes the fundraising discipline and creates the environment for its success

Nonprofits are very reluctant to take many cues from the business world but having both air and ground attacks is no longer just a consideration—it's a necessity for organizations that are wanting to do *more* good.

So Consider This a Wake-up Call!

Neglecting to market your nonprofit is doing your development department and your organization a disservice. Any good development professional will agree that great marketing creates the environment for them to be more successful. And when they work seamlessly together, the results are nearly always exponentially better.

CHAPTER 4

Five Stages of Marketing Accountability for Nonprofits

Remember the scenario I gave you in chapter 2 of someone needing a job and doing activities that seemed good, but who was failing to take the necessary steps to secure a job?

That's how many nonprofit organizations appear to marketing experts. The one thing every nonprofit needs most is to generate support so they can continue doing good work. But too often, it seems as if they're doing everything *but* the one thing they need to do to grow and thrive...and to get the *funds*!

In other words, nonprofits usually have an ongoing plan around direct-ask fundraising, but they have no marketing accountability for generating the awareness and interest they need at the top of the sales funnel so they can get the sustainable results needed at the bottom of the funnel.

Based on seeing this pattern again and again, I've developed an easy way to identify where your organization may be in terms of truly being responsible and wise about using its resources to maintain and grow its returns and impact.

Five Stages of Marketing Accountability

Take a look at these five stages and assess your organization. Like a multistep intervention program, this is a way to "look in the mirror" to see where you are . . . and make a plan, if necessary, to dig your way out:

Stage 1: Denial

If your organizational leaders question the need for marketing or avoid making an investment in it, they're most likely in denial. They refuse to believe that organizations need marketing to survive and thrive. And they don't believe their organization needs, or would benefit from, a stronger identity, improved relationships, and greater trust. As a result, denial is probably holding back your organization's growth and impact.

Stage 2: Fear

When nonprofits start running short of volunteers and/or funds, that's when they often wake up to the need for marketing. Desperate times are not the ideal backdrop for desperate marketing measures. If you wait until your back is against the wall, your options may be limited. On the other hand, being proactive with your marketing plan is similar to the conventional wisdom that it's best to go job hunting while you're still employed—you simply have more flexibility and leverage.

Stage 3: Confusion

Because so many nonprofits are unaware that they need marketing until they fear their financial support or volunteer base is drying up, their dire circumstances usually cloud their thinking. As a result, basic marketing questions that should have been resolved when the organization was formed or during routine planning meetings become bewilderingly complex. Who do we talk to? How do we talk to them? What should we say? For an organization that views marketing as a priority, well-honed answers to these questions are already in place. For the organization that lacks marketing accountability, these key elements can become complicated and very confusing.

Stage 4: Self-Promotion

Once fear and confusion have set in, there's often little room left for sound reasoning. I've frequently quoted a phrase from the early Greek soldier and poet, Archilochus, that pertains to this:

> In the face of fear, "We do not rise to the level of our expectations, instead we fall to the level of our training."[3]

When it comes to marketing, I've seen organizations in "panic mode" fall to the level of "tried-and-tired" marketing activities instead of daring to take new risks. The result is often the following:

1. Let's have an event or send out an emergency direct mail piece…
2. That (event or mailer) will give us a platform to talk about ourselves…
3. Let's hope things change as a result…

The bottom line is: "Hope" is not a good strategy.

Stage 5: Accountability

An organization with its marketing priorities properly positioned realizes that funding or revenue always *starts* with marketing awareness. And that organization also knows marketing begins with the goal of building new relationships and reinforcing existing ones. Its leaders understand that if they don't build connections with others over time, they're basically relegated to begging from strangers (in other words, panhandling, which obviously isn't an ideal way to present their brand). The reality is that for responsible organizations, marketing should always be a priority.

So take heart, there's great honor in accountability, which allows an organization to expand so that it can accomplish its mission . . . and *more*!

What about your organization—where do you fall in this spectrum? Do you need to enter a 12-step recovery program on marketing accountability? Do you need a marketing planner's intervention? Or are you stuck in a state of denial? Go ahead, say it:

"I'm [fill in your organization's name], and I have a marketing problem."

Great news: There's a lot in this book to help you through this, and soon, you'll be sober-minded and on your way to putting the pieces together to do more good.

CHAPTER 5

Five Words I Hate the Most

"We're the Best-Kept Secret"

These five words have been spoken in almost every initial meeting I've ever had with a nonprofit client. When I give workshops and seminars on the subject of nonprofit branding, someone in the audience always utters these five words. Sometimes this phrase is stated with a tinge of frustration. Often it's verbalized with some sense of shame. More often, this sentence is declared emphatically— with pride!

An attitude of frustration or shame is understandable. But to say this phrase with pride is completely confusing, and, frankly, misguided.

Not only are these words a sign of failure, they're also a badge of irresponsibility. As such, I believe it is essential that nonprofit organizations—and their leaders—understand what branding and marketing are and why they're important to the viability and vitality of their organization. You don't want to be a best-kept secret! Not only will you undermine your organization's growth, but you'll also limit its impact as well. You want the world to know what you're doing and take notice! Without support you not only don't have an organization, but an important need will go unmet, or people will continue to suffer, or something or someone will cease to exist. So when it comes to getting the attention and support your cause needs, ignoring or not deploying best practices is not just unfortunate—it's irresponsible.

So What Is Branding? And Does It Work for Nonprofits?

When it comes to branding, most nonprofit leaders want to ask the preceding two questions. In my experience, most won't ask the first question, "So what is branding?" because they believe they should or already do know about the topic. The second question, "And does it work for nonprofits?" is one they wish they had an answer for. But if they're honest with themselves, they have always struggled with it because they can't articulate an answer to the first question.

For whatever reason, branding is one of the least understood, but most important, organizational functions. Adding to the confusion, aspects of branding are known by several names that many would claim are interchangeable: marketing, development, fundraising, public relations, advertising, and communication, just to name a few.

Far too often, branding is seen as synonymous with a logo or a name. People who tend to use this definition are usually myopic in their approach to marketing and don't realize that the process of becoming a brand and maintaining that status is multidimensional.

But make no mistake, other than the services rendered by a nonprofit or faith-based organization, branding or becoming a brand name is the lifeblood of any successful organization.

In the Organizational Growth Food Chain, Branding Sits on Top

As I've often said to help people understand the difference between marketing and branding, "Marketing *does* something; a brand *is* something."

That concept can be applied to all the other labels typically given to branding efforts: advertising, communications, public relations, and fundraising. They all *do* something, but they all also serve, impact, and build a brand. And a brand is the sum of all the contacts, connections, and content created on the organization's behalf.

The marketing faculty of Kellogg School of Management at Northwestern University have another take on branding in their book *Kellogg on Branding:* "A brand is a set of associations linked to a name, mark or symbol . . . ." They continue their definition to include "a brand is much like a reputation."[4]

When a brand is framed in this way—as an organization's reputation—it's hard to argue that branding and all its service components (marketing, advertising, PR, development, and social media) are not fundamental to an organization's success! Yet organizations seem to put many other priorities ahead of branding.

Are Branding and Marketing Expenses—or Investments?

"Because the purpose of business is to create a customer, the business enterprise has two—and only two—basic functions: marketing and innovation. Marketing and innovation produce results; all the rest are costs," wrote management guru Peter Drucker.[5]

What I like about Drucker's statement is not just that he elevates marketing and innovation to a high level of importance. I like that he does so from a management perspective. He was not a "marketing guy," or an "advertising creative," or a "PR practitioner." He had no agenda or bias other than to say that marketing and innovation are the underlying goals of any organization. Everything else, he said, exists to support an organization's ability to carry out its primary purpose: to create a customer.

In short, Drucker says that people in human resources, accounting, and management are *costs*, much like buildings, supplies, and utilities. They're costs of providing an organization's services. On the other hand, marketing and innovation are investments into supporting all costs and growing the organization.

In marketing terms, though, product and service innovations are also a function of marketing. So if you look at Drucker's quote in this way, an organization only has *one* function . . . and that is marketing. And given that marketing is a component serving the brand, I believe that branding is the ultimate function of any organization.

If a for-profit organization's primary purpose is to create a customer, then a nonprofit organization's primary purpose is to create a supporter.

Deposits and Withdrawals

When organizations understand branding and marketing as an investment and a vital core responsibility, they will then be equipped to grow their organization and grow their impact.

Like any investment portfolio, these activities need to be managed well and undertaken with a balanced approach. What I see among many organizations is that they tend to overuse activities that raise funds and underinvest in communications that grow their brand.

This is easy to spot in the consumer world with retailers that scream "SALE!" every weekend. After a while, they tend to lose customer loyalty and sales (not to mention, believability and credibility) and ultimately, their business declines once strong competitors come in and match them in the price war. Smart retailers, on the other hand, build loyalty and customer preference based on differentiation. While Walmart has the lowest prices, Target is seen as being cooler by a coveted target audience known as "healthy, wealthy moms."

In the nonprofit world, "always a crisis" donation campaigns are equivalent to those retailers yelling "SALE!" If nonprofits don't build trust, differentiation, and emotional connections, they won't create loyalty, bonds, and advocacy.

Any large business or nonprofit that successfully grows and becomes a brand typically manages their marketing or fundraising investments with the understanding that some activities and efforts are "deposits" while others are "withdrawals."

In fact, all the big retailers I know use this same model: 30 percent of their advertising budget is spent on "brand" and 70 percent is spent on "promotion."

They know that brand advertising, sometimes called "image" advertising, is not necessarily going to drive traffic through their door, but it's critical in order to keep their brand differentiation bank account funded and balanced.

They see branding as a "deposit" so they'll have money on reserve to "withdraw" when needed in the future.

In the nonprofit world, those "withdrawals" include all high-pressure fundraising tactics. The organization needs to make "deposits" so there is something there to withdraw. Making a "deposit" means communicating with your donors that they're doing something significant by being engaged in your mission; they can feel good about themselves!

Then, when you do ask them for a donation, the "deposit" is already there to withdraw, and you have saved up enough brand equity in your brand bank account for them to say, "Yes, I understand; now it's time to make a withdrawal."

Withdrawals include all marketing and fundraising efforts that include an "ask." Whether that's through direct mail, online giving opportunities, social media posts, events, or gatherings, all such ask activities are leveraging your brand for support.

Deposits are the activities that build your brand and create loyalty: storytelling, connecting without an agenda, providing updates on outcomes, educating, and sharing your organization's unique approaches and differences made.

Like any financial portfolio, you must be careful not to overdraw your account and maintain a healthy balance between your deposits and withdrawals.

So back to the formula used by retailers: Think about 30 percent of your investments being sizable deposits and 70 percent being smaller withdrawals. You may ask, how is that a balanced approach? Note this ratio is the amount of effort, not the amount of investment. It's a qualitative rather than a quantitative ratio. Which is to say, the consumer world understands that when you make a deposit, it should be big, strong, impactful, and emotional so it resonates and reverberates within and throughout your withdrawal efforts!

In short, your organization needs to *create* value before *extracting* it.

CHAPTER 6

Touch Every Touchpoint

Howard Schultz, founder of Starbucks, was asked how he built one of the world's largest brands with virtually no advertising. After all, brands usually become brand names by promoting themselves through massive and expensive media campaigns. Schultz is credited as saying, "Understanding branding is easy. Everything matters."[6]

What did he mean by that? Essentially, he was saying that an organization makes an imprint with each contact a person has with that brand—whether the contact is from an ad or through an experience. The key to Starbucks's success is understanding that every brand touchpoint matters to achieving customer loyalty. If you know anything about the Starbucks experience, you understand that it leaves very little to chance. From the store location, décor, signage, music, and product packaging, to the baristas working behind the counter, everything is intentional—and everything is managed as if it matters to the company's brand perceptions and its overall success. Each and every contact is managed to make the best impression possible.

Start Branding from the Inside Out

As you begin to think about strengthening your brand, a good place to start is with the "brand inside." Ask yourself and others within your organization these questions:

- What does our signage, location, and even our reception area say about our organization?
- When someone calls or stops by our office, how are they treated?
- When our volunteers or staff send emails, leave voicemails, or answer the phone, how do they come across?
- What kind of cars do our key contacts drive? How do they dress?
- When we host a meeting of donors, volunteers, board members, or community leaders, does our agenda say, *We value your time and we have meaningful business to take care of*, or do we get lost in minutia?
- How do our volunteers, staff, leaders, and board members talk about our organization to their families and friends and in their comments on social media?
- Do we look at everything we send out—direct mail, annual reports, email, Facebook, and Twitter updates—as a chance to make a positive impression about the good work we're doing?

Positive, Negative, or Unrealized— Which Is Worse?

Though it may seem counterintuitive, unrealized brand contacts are often worse than negative contacts. That's because a negative impression typically prompts a reaction or complaint and, thus, an opportunity for the organization to respond and turn a negative impression into a positive one. However, unrealized contacts—impressions that go completely unnoticed—fail to advance your brand in any direction.

When I speak on this topic, many people often ask me to give them an example of an unrealized brand contact. I respond by asking, "Did you watch TV last night? If so, can you remember any commercials you saw?" Can you remember one or a handful of the commercials you saw? The rest were *unrealized* brand contacts. Companies spent good money and effort to garner your attention, but they missed the mark. Those were real dollars invested, but they generated little to no return or response.

A top-level "Brand Experience" consultant with whom I once worked always asked his clients to pretend that they were a club that requires people to pay a membership fee. He then would ask:

- Why would people want to belong to this club?
- Why would they pay to get in?
- How much would their membership be worth to them?
- What would they say to get others to join?
- Why would they renew their membership?

In short, he was saying the experiences people have with a brand must be managed intentionally so they continually bring value, or return on investment. Supporters incur costs well beyond the dollars they contribute—their time, attention, and consideration are all valuable. So make every contact count.

How about your organization—are you deliberately managing every brand contact? Are you inspired to make everything matter and to put your organization in the best position to do more good?

CHAPTER 7

The 6 Ps of Nonprofit Marketing

You're probably familiar with the "4 Ps of Marketing" that have been taught in business schools for decades. These are considered the pillars of a strong marketing program. E. Jerome McCarthy was the first person to suggest the "4 Ps of Marketing,"[7] which constitute what's called a "marketing mix." This term refers to the combination of actions or tactics that a company uses to promote its brand or product in the marketplace.

In my thirty-plus-year career, I've noticed that many people, even within industries that should know better, often mistake marketing as being a mix of things such as advertising, promotions, personal selling, events, and publicity. The reality is that the marketing mix is much more complex, and those mistaken elements are all just a small part of one "P."

Just for a Quick Review, the 4 Ps Are

Product—This part of the marketing mix includes the delivery system design, technology, quality, services provided, and their availability.

Price—This silo of the marketing mix includes costs to users or supporters, payment periods, arrangements, and terms. "Costs" can be more than dollars…they can be emotional currency (for example, greater purpose, advancements, or victory), sacrificial aspects (your donors giving time, energy, or focus), and relational (what do donor associations with your organization *do* for their identity and relationships? Will people think more or less of them because they are identified with you?).

Place—An oft-overlooked part of the marketing mix, this "P" includes strategy and executional elements surrounding service distribution channels, coverage, locations, logistics, and e-services.

Promotion—The most well-known aspect of the marketing mix, this piece involves strategies and tactics related to advertising, logo/identity, and promotions. But it also covers development/fundraising, communication, events, and public relations since they are all tools in your greater marketing and branding strategy.

Since the introduction of the 4 Ps, I've heard of many different proposed additions to the marketing mix. Some have argued that "People" or "Process" should be separate elements. But the reality is, there's nothing in marketing that doesn't require a human element, and any process is likely an extension of a strategy or tactic in one of the existing 4 Ps.

And that's why the 4 Ps have endured for sixty-plus years as the key "commandments" of building a solid marketing plan. But there's more!

After many years of very careful consideration, I am now humbly suggesting that two new "Ps" be added to the marketing mix, especially for organizations that want to do *more* good (including for-profit corporations and businesses with a bent toward social responsibility and making an impact).

Those Two New Ps Are Participation and Purpose

Participation

Long gone are the days of using only mass media through limited outlets to drive awareness, discussion, commerce, and contributions. Those times of three television networks and a few daily newspapers are so far in the rearview mirror of communication history, there are likely only a few people reading this now who remember them (or will admit it, if they do)!

Media and how we communicate with one another are no longer simply about "mass" forms of communications. While you still can't underestimate the power of television (which is being consumed at its highest levels ever and is still the dominant media preferred by the greatest number of adult Americans,[8]) newspaper outlets such as *The New York Times* and *The Washington Post* are thriving in digital form. The "new media" isn't new anymore. Facebook, Instagram, Twitter, and YouTube are now as respected, utilized, and ingrained in our culture as any traditional media channels from our past.

Bullhorn types of marketing approaches focused on one-way communication are now less accepted, influential, and impactful. Today's media and communication demand interactivity, not just through words and digital channels, but with physical presence and action. Your donors need to see firsthand the good work that your organization is doing!

Instead of "preaching" to people and throwing information at them on social media—pose an intriguing question and ask people to answer it. How much more engagement would you get if you welcomed people to participate in the conversation?

Child Sponsorships Are a
Great Example of This "P"

When donors participate in child sponsorship, they connect with the children they support. They vicariously share what's happening in the lives of "their" children, but World Vision, a global poverty relief organization, is also very good at bringing its high-net-worth donors to meet the children it sponsors to experience their lives for themselves.

I talked with one high-level World Vision donor and asked him, "Why do you support World Vision?" He said, "They brought me to a village where I got to see a well tapped for the first time in a community that didn't have clean water. I got to see it for myself . . . the well I made possible through my donation . . . I got to see the impact it made on the people there, and I'll never forget that."

If World Vision's donors can meet the people and see the villages that they are helping firsthand—that's participation!

Habitat for Humanity is a nationally renowned nonprofit that builds houses for low income and homeless people. It's also the king of participation. Once it gets you out there swinging a hammer, it has you! For the rest of your life, you can say, "I helped build a Habitat for Humanity home," even if it was only for a day or half a day.

In fact, that participation is so important to its model that it tells politicians, celebrities, and famous athletes, "We don't want your money! We only want you to show up at one of our events where people are actively building a home and swing a hammer for fifteen minutes so we get good photos and video of you doing that; that's all we want from you."

The organization is very smart—it knows that a participating celebrity, politician, or athlete makes people say, "Look, Tim Tebow or Jimmy Carter came, and they swung a hammer!" And that motivates so many more people to support the organization and who'll want to get out there to help build a house themselves.

While this was true prior to the COVID-19 pandemic, personal participation has become even more desired because of it. People don't just want to give their money to a cause—they want to be identified with it and connected to it.

Social media intertwined with social distancing has and will heighten the trend for engagement and involvement. Organizations need to understand that their brand isn't just owned by them; it is owned by all who associate themselves with it. Today personal brands are important, and people's associations and support define who they are more than ever.

Organizations today need to see themselves as media channels, constantly transmitting a voice for a cause. And they need to see their audiences as citizen journalists and content contributors to their own media channels. That means organizational communications and marketing need to give your audiences opportunity to express themselves and communicate how they feel about your brand. Sometimes that's with words or investigating events for themselves. Sometimes that's connecting and networking with you and others who are like-minded.

The need for participation, connection, and engagement has been escalating for years. COVID-19 has made these things more difficult for an extended period; therefore, connection and participation are more valuable. In fact, these attributes have become a marketing necessity!

Purpose

Purpose is the sixth "P" of marketing. I think we'd all agree that a well-defined, focused, and emotive purpose is not only important for an organization, it has also become extremely desirable. Everyone who comes into contact with a group or service today wants their organization to have a clear and compelling purpose. This goes for staff, volunteers, donors, and those who are served.

With so many good choices today and so much noise in the marketplace tugging at our discretionary time, money, attention, and resources, organizations with a true, meaningful, and purpose-powered difference stand out.

I've often said that a memorable and sustainable brand is more than a logo, location, website, or campaign—it's about the perceptions you create and the promises you make (and keep).

I believe "Purpose" is the most powerful element of any marketing mix since it can and should be the driver of every other aspect (and every other "P").

Discovering and/or better defining your purpose requires a multistep process. The goal is to create a singular, purpose-powered strategic vision that is fact-based, unique, relevant, and compelling.

Following are a few key steps you can utilize to develop a powerful purpose statement for your nonprofit organization:

Step 1: Brainstorm with your team to develop your organization's Value Proposition. Here are some topics to discuss:

- Who, or what, does your organization serve?
- What is it that you really do as a service?
- What makes your organization or your service unique, special, or better than others?

Your findings will populate a value proposition equation like this:

- **The sum of:** Who or what you serve, what you do, and what makes this service unique, special, or better than what other organizations are doing.
- **Equals:** Your Value Proposition

WHO DO YOU SERVE?

WHAT DO YOU DO?

WHAT MAKES YOU UNIQUE?

Value Proposition

Step 2: Use your answers to the previous three questions to look for the interconnections between what is "true, meaningful, and different" about your organization. A Venn diagram like the following one can then help you to determine the core purpose that best connects these overlapping variable attributes. These circles represent these qualities: true, meaningful, and different.

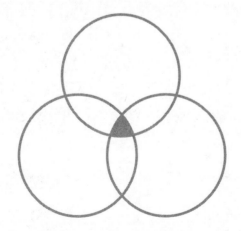

True, Meaningful + Different

**Step 3: Your nonprofit undoubtedly already has a
mission statement and a vision statement.**

Now it's time to develop a "purpose statement" by combining
the core of what is "true, meaningful, and different" about your organization and the value you deliver to who and/or what you serve.

Communicating your purpose illustrates that your organizational commitments transcend operations and functionality, and
that your concerns are centered on the positive differences you
desire and are working to make happen!

CHAPTER 8

Introduction to the IDEAS Process: So What's the Big Idea?

I remember feeling awfully intimidated at the American Advertising Federation's Hall of Achievement awards ceremony in New York City. I was sitting at a table with people who I felt were way above my pay grade.

The top Coca-Cola and IBM marketing guys were there, and many others—it was eye-opening.

I was sitting at that table with people who manage multibillion-dollar brands. I knew I didn't fit in—I was kind of the odd man out, since I was the only "cause" marketer—and they were all leading the marketing efforts of major consumer brands.

Little did I expect to be inducted into their Hall of Achievement for "Doing the Best Cause Work," but as I mentioned, the reaction of these advertising "giants" surprised me most of all!

Most people in the room—publications and media—were there to impress and congratulate these rock stars of marketing, but after I spoke, the tables kind of turned. I realized that they were aspiring to have as much contribution to the world as the nonprofits we work for do.

I heard my name, and the hosts invited me to the stage to accept the award and to say a few words. When I returned to my seat, the for-profit marketing gurus at my table said, "We feel so silly here, seeing the kind of work that YOU do . . . it's so meaningful and important . . . compared to the stuff we do."

They were kind of jealous! I realized they saw my work as equally valuable to their more glamorous and lucrative companies.

Reach higher.

The awards ceremony was held at The Plaza hotel in New York City, right across from Central Park where the movie *Home Alone* was filmed—and the ballroom had an amazing golden ceiling—just gorgeous—it was probably real gold!

I didn't plan to mention it in my acceptance speech, but I was so amazed by this golden ceiling that when I went to the podium to receive my award, I started my speech by reminiscing about an old exercise that I had been part of at a day-long seminar under a similar golden ceiling, where the organizers had placed notepads, pencils, and paper clips in the center of each table.

At that seminar, the speaker said he wanted to begin with a team-building exercise. "I want everyone to work together at your tables to build the tallest tower that you can using only the materials in the center of your table." The presenter said that for years he had conducted this same exercise, and all the winning towers were predictably about the same height . . . until one day, he happened to be in a ballroom with a beautiful ceiling like this one. His instructions changed just that one day from, "Build the tallest structure you can," to, "This ceiling is so beautiful, build a structure as close to that ceiling as you can."

And he said on *that* day, the structures at each table were the tallest he'd ever seen!

"Be careful what goals you give people," he said, "because if you give people more powerful goals, they will possibly go higher than they've ever been able to before."

Big IDEAS Are Key

Many marketing and branding people today prefer to talk about things such as digital media, social media, and mobile applications—these are the buzzwords we read and hear about every day in the hype that surrounds our craft. Yet as far as I can figure, no one has yet come up with a powerful form of communication that does not at least begin as a big idea.

Big ideas create greater outcomes and unstoppable momentum. And that's the goal of the brand development system I've developed based on the **IDEAS** Process. The process flows like this:

- **Insights** – In this phase, we start by questioning and asking what leads to pivotal knowledge and provides the basis for confident action.
- **Direction** – During this phase, it is important to determine and design integrated solutions for specific goals and objectives.
- **Expression** – Now it's time to explore creative storytelling options that focus on developing messaging (both verbal and visual) to create a stronger and more differentiated brand. The goal is conception driven by compelling communication that moves audiences to your brand in ways that are meaningful to them.
- **Action** – Then we need to generate a responsive "go-to market" approach, through strategy and careful planning, that positively impacts every key audience you want to reach, at every brand touchpoint.
- **Success** – Here we look for ways to measure and optimize the investments made and leverage progress, looking to yield better outcomes and create unstoppable momentum.

What Makes This Idea Different?

I have personally found from decades of utilizing the IDEAS Process that this approach provides more highly strategic and customized solutions to organizational marketing issues and opportunities than other techniques I've seen implemented.

Unlike the processes of many other organizations, agencies, and consultants that service the nonprofit community, the **IDEAS** Process is not about "boilerplate" or "off-the-shelf" solutions. The organizations that offer these types of services have very predictable outcomes, and they also have a very predictable pattern of locking nonprofit organizations into never-ending programs that ultimately have diminishing returns, cause donor fatigue, and have dismal relationship retention rates.

I shared with you about my night spent at the Mel Trotter Mission, and my story of being "homeless for a day" illustrates these points well.

It all started with **Insights**—that's why I slept at the mission overnight and, as a result, discovered insights that shaped and drove our messaging.

Then there was **Direction**—my team and I had to put together a plan of attack based on what we knew—what their goals were and what we understood about the marketplace and competitive forces.

Expression was next—the plan had to be executed through the creative to express their brand in powerful and attention-commanding ways.

And then **Action**—we went to market, we did things that nonprofits at the time were not doing (they were all primarily using direct mail and banquets), and we directed the Mel Trotter Mission not to do direct mail or banquets. Instead it should take the budgeted funds for those programs and put them toward TV, outdoor, and newspaper advertising.

So let's take a look at the way we measured this campaign's **Success.**

The rescue mission's leader, Rev. Layman, said, "Bill, all you've got to do is beat three-to-one—that's the ROI we're currently bringing in when we do direct mail or a banquet. But you guys are telling me that three-to-one is a low bar. So go for it!"

As luck would have it, we didn't start on the Mel Trotter Ministries campaign until October, so we didn't have a lot of running room before its critical fundraising peak season between Thanksgiving and Christmas. We did everything as planned and yet, by the end of the year, the mission had only gotten a two-to-one return on investment.

This caused Rev. Layman to pay an unannounced visit to our offices. He literally walked from the rescue mission and virtually kicked down our front office door (as you can imagine, there's no worse feeling than having a reverend from a rescue mission mad at you!). He said, "Bill, you told me that a three-to-one return stinks, but you only delivered two-to-one!"

I said, "Reverend, you forgot one detail—I also said that it takes six to eighteen months to build a brand. We just got started. And the fact that you got two-to-one in this short timeframe—I'm kind of amazed."

He said, "Yeah, but what am I supposed to tell my board of directors?"

I said, "Tell your board to measure us a year from now! Don't measure us after only two months."

And a year from that date, their return was nine-to-one—and it continued to grow from there, until the folks at Mel Trotter just stopped counting!

The **IDEAS** Process takes its approach from the actions of what the biggest and most prolific brands in the world do to grow their businesses. Basically, my goal is to teach you their secrets and help you and your organization succeed. Using this IDEAS Process, you can create a unique position in the minds and hearts of your key support audiences, and over time, that will yield significantly better outcomes and help to create more meaningful brand relationships. It's like a success ripple effect that extends and grows your organization for years.

That's why the marketing gurus at the AAF Awards in New York were envious. Not only was I helping worthy causes, but together with my nonprofit clients we were outsmarting, not outspending, the consumer market and attracting more than our fair share of people's discretionary time and money because we had better **IDEAS**.

That's what we'll explore in the next few chapters. I will not only walk you through how the IDEAS Process works and flows, I'll provide you with tools, best practices, strategies, and approaches for taking your messaging, marketing, and branding to higher levels. As such, you'll have what you need to get your cause the attention and differentiation it needs and deserves.

PART II

INSIGHTS

IDEAS PROCESS
I = Insights

Doing nonprofit work for controversial causes is challenging because I have high standards about maintaining a civil discourse. It's vital to present your beliefs and values in a manner that's honest, sincere, respectful, and allows people to make informed choices.

I always want my side to win, but even more, I want to be proud of how we win. I've found that winning in these campaigns is often about finding a key insight that gives you a competitive advantage.

This was the case when I was working for one side of two notoriously opposed forces: one was pro this and the other was pro that. As far as both sides were concerned, there was no middle ground.

However, when we did our research with a key younger target audience that both groups wanted to influence, we found that *neither* side was trusted by this audience since *both* were seen as too political and divisive.

With that insight, we tested a lot of messaging on its ability to change hearts and minds while staying above the divisive political fray. Curiously, it was factual information that the opponents were sharing that proved to be the most compelling messaging. Unfortunately for our opponents, the facts they were sharing worked against them, not for them.

Once we discovered these insights, we were able to create what we called a "Pro-Knowledge" campaign. By staying apolitical and presenting repackaged facts originally expressed by the opponents, we were able to form a new indisputable narrative and make significant inroads within a coveted target group.

Without the benefit of these insights, I'm sure we would have been much less effective—and we would have likely stoked more fires and created greater division. And that wouldn't have been good for either side.

CHAPTER 9

Critical Questions

Question Everything

For more than thirty years I've been asking organizations I work with to fill out a set of "critical questions" to help us quickly gauge the marketing landscape and general brand health of their organization. These critical questions allow me and my colleagues to dig a bit deeper into an organization's market and competition while gathering insights into their marketing communication priorities. More often than not, simply asking these questions reveals answers to current problems and missed opportunities. I want to share a sample with you.

Question Everyone

I've also made it standard practice to ask multiple stakeholders within an organization to answer critical questions individually, without comparing notes. We ask them not to discuss the questions with anyone and to submit their answers directly to us. The divergent perspectives we receive often give us additional insight, such as the fact that everyone might not be on the same page.

My guess is that if you ask multiple stakeholders within your own organization—such as the executive director, fundraising director, board chairperson, and volunteer coordinator—to answer these questions, you'll also discover some critical insights.

Following is a list of some of the questions you might use for this task:

Organizational Background

1. What sets your organization apart from other organizations providing the same or similar services? (Or those soliciting the same donors and volunteers?)
2. What should be the primary marketing objectives for your organization in the coming year? For the next three years? (Maybe these include building name recognition and awareness, repositioning your organization, increasing donor activity, recruiting more volunteers, or adding new partnerships.)
3. What are three strengths and three weaknesses of your organization's branding and marketing efforts right now?

Market Situation

4. What are three trends currently impacting your organization? (Perhaps the social/political climate, increasing/decreasing community need, aging constituency or donor base, or geographic/international nuances.)

Competitive Situation

5. Who or what do you consider to be your primary competitors? (Other organizations providing the same or similar services and/or targeting the same or similar donors or volunteers? "Competition" can also be things such as apathy or distractions that compete for people's time, attention, and money—such as the mall, movie theater, sporting events, or theme parks.)
6. What are these competitors doing or saying that you perceive to be successful from a marketing and communications standpoint?

7. How can your organization differentiate itself from these competitors?

Target Audience

8. Identify and rank the audiences most crucial to your success.
9. What are their current attitudes regarding your organization?
10. Why does your organization matter to these target audiences?

Opportunities and Barriers

11. What are the main marketing opportunities that your organization should be emphasizing?
12. What are the main obstacles to overcome for your marketing efforts to be successful?

Marketing and Communications

13. Do you believe that your organization proactively (vs. reactively) manages its brand? Please explain.
14. What marketing and communication efforts have worked well for your organization in the past?
15. What marketing and communication efforts have *not* worked well for your organization in the past?

These questions—and the answers received—can be useful to get an initial read on the marketing landscape and brand health of your organization. By asking multiple stakeholders to answer these questions, you can discover great insights critical to advancing your organization's brand and marketing success. That's why we call them the "critical questions."

What's Your Take?

Have you ever asked multiple stakeholders to answer similar questions? Are you and the major stakeholders in your organization on the same page when it comes to marketing opportunities? If you've gone through these questions, how have the answers you gathered provided insights—and are there any recurring themes or points that are easily connected?

This is where your efforts get exciting because wrestling with these weighty questions can reveal new "discoveries" that will improve your marketing plan for the future. Let's keep going!

CHAPTER 10

Research Fundamentals: Seven Things Nonprofits Should Know from Market Research

Knowing Your Audience Should Be a Primary Concern

The world is divided into two camps when it comes to market and brand research: those who conduct formal research and those who use informal methods. But market research is not defined by your methods, but by your sources. Those sources are either primary (research that you commission, conduct, and own) or secondary (research that other people commission, conduct, and own . . . and then make available, sometimes for a fee or as a service).

Start with Secondary Research

It may sound counterintuitive, but you should start with secondary research. This type of research is typically found through associations and/or trade publications and websites focused on your specific service area. For example, in the education market, associations that may conduct and publish secondary market research include the National Education Association, the Association of American Educators, and the National Home Education Research Institute. Publications that conduct and publish secondary education research include *Education Week* and *Home Education Magazine*.

Even if there are not associations and publications that focus on your specific service area, numerous nonprofit and philanthropic organizations, associations, and publications provide and publish market research that provides a good starting place.

Utilize Primary Research for Further Insights

Once you've exhausted all secondary resources for insights and information into your organization's target audiences, you will want to know more about the specific audiences you are targeting for support.

Whether you conduct your primary research informally (using mail questionnaires, phone surveys, polls at events, or an online tool such as Survey Monkey) or formally (using a research firm or department to gather responses through focus groups or surveys of the general public), gathering insights about your target audiences is critical to being a good steward of your marketing investment.

Seven Audience Insights You Should Learn from Market Research

There's a lot you could ask your target audience, but you should first ask yourself, *What is it that I really need to know?*

From my perspective, there are seven essential audience insights:

1. **Awareness measurement**—The most informative awareness research is conducted by surveying those who do not currently support your organization. When conducting research among non-supporting audiences, awareness questions should be among the first ones asked, even before favorable/unfavorable ratings. There are two basic measurements of awareness: "unaided," in which respondents are asked to list organization names without any prompting, and "aided," which prompts respondents with a list of organization names to see which ones they've heard of before. When measuring awareness, you should do one "benchmark" study before you launch a new marketing or branding initiative. Then conduct one more survey as a follow-up to the initiative so you can compare their results. By measuring public awareness before and after a marketing effort, you'll be able to understand whether or not the campaign actually improved recognition of your organization.

2. **Favorable and unfavorable ratings**—How do people perceive your organization? Do they have a favorable impression or an unfavorable one? Or do they have no impression at all? When asking questions in this area, be sure to compare yourself to other organizations that offer the same or similar services. If there are no other similar organizations, compare yourself to respected as "gold standard" nonprofits such as The Salvation Army, Goodwill Industries, and the American Red Cross—they all tend to have high favorable ratings.

3. **Purpose Playback**—Gaining awareness of your organization's primary purpose is often the bridge from being known to being supported. Obviously your donors need to know your purpose, and that purpose needs to resonate with them. If enough people know your organization's name

and know why it exists, you're clearly on the road to success. As with awareness research, you can ask both unaided and aided questions to assess knowledge of your primary purpose and see if respondents can actually "play it back" for you. Similar to awareness measurements, it's a good idea to get a benchmark number on "purpose playback" prior to launching a new marketing initiative, and then compare it to the number achieved following the initiative.

4. **Success Statement Scoring**—Most organizations want to accomplish more than one objective. And most organizations provide more than one program or service to accomplish those objectives. In short, every organization should understand and be able to define what "victory" or "success" looks like and how they plan to achieve it. Write down your objectives, programs, and services, and ask donors and potential supporters to rate their importance (such as "very important," "somewhat important," "neutral," "somewhat unimportant," or "not at all important"). Once you tally those scores, you'll gain insight into what your organization does that resonates best with supporters and potential supporters.

5. **Top Proposition Testing**—Propositions are statements about your organization that you use or would likely use to persuade others to support your organization. Most are built around a singular assumption: If someone only knew this *one* thing about your organization, would they be likely to support it? When testing or researching propositions, it's best to phrase those propositions using generic language without flowery phrasing or marketing hype. In other words, just give people the facts in as straightforward a manner as possible.

You can "gussy up" the language later, but people tend to be skeptical of marketing language and might not respond honestly if they sense any hype. When researching various propositions, it's good to arrange and test them in categories. For example, test "service" propositions or "outcome" propositions as a batch. Usually, I test fifteen to twenty-five propositions when conducting this type of research and ask respondents to score each one on a scale of whether a statement makes them more or less likely to support an organization (that is, "much more likely," "somewhat more likely," "no difference, "somewhat less likely," "much less likely," or "don't know").

Once the results are in, you should rank your propositions from highest to lowest scoring. The top three to five propositions should always be part of your marketing communications. As for the bottom three to five propositions—it's probably a good idea to avoid those.

6. **Media Habits:** It's often difficult to discern the best way to reach your target—unless, of course, you ask them. A basic question to ask in any research effort is how your organization can best communicate information. A simple example might be: "If we wanted to reach you and others like you, what ways would work best?" Be sure to have a comprehensive "prompt" list that includes email, radio, TV, billboards, direct mail, newsletters, social media, church, or school. If someone gives you a "media" answer, be sure to get a few specifics—what radio station, TV network, and program do you like or prefer? These kinds of questions are always good to ask donors or those who call your organization on a continuous basis. Just a simple, "How did you hear about us?" is also a good barometer for locations or platforms your organization should consider for messaging, public relations, or advertising.

7. **Demographic Profiles**—No study is complete without
   gathering basic demographic information such as age range,
   gender, education level, marital status, geographic location,
   and income categories. Other good demographic information items to gather are donor status (past/current/none),
   religiosity (attend church regularly, sometimes, or not at all),
   and affiliations (such as Evangelical, Protestant, Catholic,
   Jewish, Muslim, Mormon, or other).

A good tip came from a friend of mine, Josh McQueen, the
former EVP of research and planning for Leo Burnett and a guest
speaker at the inaugural DO MORE GOOD National Conference. He
said that you should always use ranges with even numbers. Instead
of a five- or seven-point scale, use a four- or six-point scale. This is
important because nearly every researcher I know says the opposite. Josh's experience, from literally doing millions upon millions
of surveys, leads him to believe that giving people a "neutral choice"
in the middle is a cop-out. That answer will be chosen often even
if people have an opinion one way or the other. He believes people
don't want to think that hard to make a choice in a survey or they're
too nice to say something bad, so they default to the neutral option
(the middle choice on a scale with an odd number of points). But
you want survey respondents to tell you which way they're leaning,
so an even point scale with no middle choice produces more honest
results.

The bottom line: Research provides knowledge. And the more
you know, the more you reduce the risk of failure and increase the
opportunity for success.

CHAPTER 11

Competitive Analysis: Why Sizing Up Your Nonprofit "Competition" Matters

"Competition" is a tough word to frame in the nonprofit world. But the reality is that whether you have direct competitors (organizations that provide the same or similar services as your organization) or indirect competitors (organizations that appeal to the same audiences as your organization), every nonprofit is in competition for the discretionary time, attention, resources, and money of others.

That's why **differentiation** is critical. For clarity, *differentiation* is articulating why your organization has a sustainable competitive advantage.

A Different Way to Differentiate

Differentiating your organization can be a difficult task, especially if you attempt to do it in a vacuum. An important step—and one that many organizations skip—is to identify competitive *gaps* in the marketplace. That means identifying what your competitors are *not* doing or *not* saying about what they do to meet the needs of the people they serve.

When I've conducted competitive reviews of differentiated positions taken by my client's competitors, the opportunity gaps have frequently become blatantly obvious. We've discovered that if you take time to review what your competitors are saying about themselves and what they offer, your own organization's uniqueness will likely become extremely clear.

Even if you don't believe you have "competition," you can still use the following tool to examine other category leaders (organizations like yours from around the country that you view as having strong communications efforts) and analyze what they are saying about themselves. Then use that knowledge to analyze what you're saying to see if there is a "gap" that no one else is filling.

The following "Competitive Review Matrix" is an excellent tool to help identify opportunities for differentiation within your overall service category and between individual offerings:

ENTITY	DIFFERENTIATION	BENEFITS OFFERED

As an example, here is a completed matrix about the competitors of a nonprofit private higher-education institution:

INSTITUTION	INSTITUTIONAL DIFFERENTIATION	EDUCATIONAL POSITIONING
Prestigious Private College	Scholarly research, informed and creative teaching, and service to the community and society at large.	Seeks to advance human well-being by fostering greater learning.
State-Run University	A national model of an engaged university employing intellectual resources and enriching lives.	Prepares qualified practitioners to be professional leaders in various educational roles.
Technical University	A welcoming campus, affordable education, a successful career, and a challenging environment — we'll take you there.	Produces competent, caring professionals for a diverse technological society.

The educational nonprofit I was working with saw the "gaps" that were identified within their competitive set. From the ones listed in this chart, we saw there were opportunity gaps in personal relevancy and authentic empowerment. The competitive institutions focused on what the college would do for the student and not what the student would do within their environment. They make the school the hero, not the students and professors.

As a result, their institutional differentiation became focused on being "A national leader in equipping students to make an impact in the world." Their program positioning became centered on "A philosophy of creative engagement of students and professors, including constructive introspection, to dream big and accomplish more."

Compared to the client's competition, this positioning is unmistakably different. And the results of our efforts demonstrated the effectiveness of this approach.

Different Is Better than Better

Differentiation is often underestimated. I find many organizations strive for excellence, believing that their *quality* is their differentiator. The reality is, quality and doing your best are already *expected* by your audiences!

When I speak on this topic, I remind my audiences that marketing is not about putting information before the public and expecting that to lead to their support. Marketing is about differentiation and positioning. And given that, a better product or service doesn't always produce a dominant category leader.

I often demonstrate this in my talks by asking some simple questions that make this point painfully obvious, such as, "Is Walmart the best store you've ever shopped in? Is McDonald's the best food you've ever had at a restaurant? If you're a beer drinker, is Budweiser the best beer you've ever had?"

Almost nobody says these brands are the *best*. But they are recognized as the biggest successes in their respective categories, and they're seen as the best marketers. These brands stand out in the crowd because they emphasize their differences. And by differentiating and distancing themselves from their competitors, they have found great advantages in achieving growth and success.

Have you clearly identified your organization's competition? Has your organization reviewed what its competition says about itself? And if so, how has it helped you differentiate *your* message?

CHAPTER 12

Product Definition: What's the "Product" of Your Nonprofit?

What Your Organization Provides Defines Its "Product"

Most nonprofits don't believe they're in the product game. They prefer to think of themselves as "service providers" or "humanitarian organizations."

Yet many experts see how marketing—even for nonprofits—revolves around having a distinguishable **product**. When your product, service, or organization is unique, and ideally, a "game changer," then marketing and fundraising become a lot easier...and a lot less expensive!

Well-known author and blogger Seth Godin started this conversation with a post and diagram about "The Circles of Marketing."[9] He argues that if a product, service, or organization is remarkable to start with, much of its marketing or fundraising will virtually take care of itself. Its uniqueness will result in usability and support ... leading to a "story" in the community as a "tribe" is developing its loyal followers ... and soon the "buzz" and "hype" will be grassroots and result in social media clicks, public relations interest, and, in general, "getting the word out" to the public about your product, service, or organization.

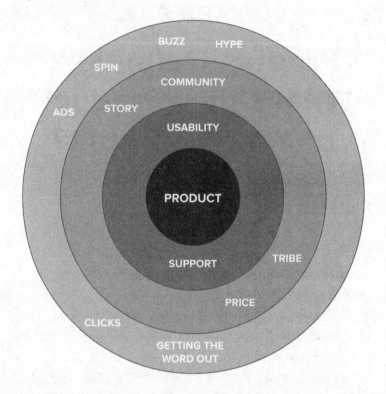

Another blogger, The Agitator,[10] highlights Godin's "Circles of Marketing" and notes that marketing and fundraising professionals rarely get the opportunity to shape, much less invent, the organizational "product" they're selling. As a result, fundraisers and marketers, he says, "can only do so much to make a nonprofit more appealing."[11] (Note: The Agitator does allude to something close to "inherent drama" by talking about "organizational virtues" and the need to make those "shine forth" in all communications. But in this post, The Agitator did not make it clear that to "know" these virtues often requires a lot of digging, not to mention the confidence that there's almost always a treasure to be unearthed when you have the knowledge and skills to do it.)

Both Godin and The Agitator Are Correct—But Not Completely Correct

Your nonprofit is only a commodity if you let it be one.

Regardless of whether nonprofits see what they provide (and how they provide it) as a "product" or not, I believe there's an important takeaway from both bloggers: Anytime you can create something unique, your marketing efforts are enhanced and naturally become simpler!

What Godin and The Agitator are *missing*, however, is that *every* organization has something called "inherent drama." It's something they do, say, support, devise, or put out that already gets them the attention, support, and loyalty they currently enjoy. "Inherent drama" means that the organization has characteristics that cause people to identify with it and get behind it. For example, consumers know that a Hallmark card can express the emotions they are feeling for a person or occasion. They don't need to be convinced by an advertising campaign to purchase them.

This means that if your organization already has supporters now, there's probably good reason for it. That reason could be the way you do things. Or the results you achieve. Or how you train your people or engage supporters. Or you may have a CEO or executive director who can communicate very effectively. Or it may be the fact that your overall vision is incredibly compelling.

The bottom line is that *every* organization has some aspect or attribute that *already* makes it remarkable! Sometimes it just takes a little more probing and soul-searching to uncover it. And this book, especially over the next five or six chapters, has plenty of ways and suggestions on how to do that . . . and do more good as a result.

— PART III —

DIRECTION

IDEAS PROCESS
D = Direction

Marketing in a new direction, deploying tactics not used before, may bring unexpected challenges. That was the case when I recommended that a rescue mission run a TV campaign instead of using their tried-and-tired tactic of guilt-inducing direct mail.

I vividly remember the executive director of the rescue mission barging into my office. Before he could settle down, he blurted out, "Nice work, Bill. You convinced me to run TV commercials, and the first one you create is now going to get banned from TV!" I had no clue what he was ranting about, but like a typical marketing guy, I wondered if there wasn't a great PR opportunity in getting banned!

He told me that a local TV station was getting complaints about our ad. Those calls were being answered by the station's receptionist, who was a supporter of the mission, and she was the one who gave him a "heads up" that momentum was building to pull the ad. I immediately called the receptionist, and she said viewers claimed the ads were "disturbing." I asked if she'd do me a favor. "Please tell people who call that it's *supposed* to be disturbing—it's an ad about homelessness." Then I asked her to see how people responded before passing their complaints to the station manager.

Later that day I checked in with her to see how it was going. She let me know that she was enjoying telling people that they should be disturbed ... and disturbed enough to help the mission fight homelessness. And she informed me that none of the callers had asked to speak to the station manager so we shouldn't worry about being banned from their channel.

Had we been stopped in our effort, the cost wouldn't have just impacted donations. This TV ad campaign was later credited with significantly elevating public awareness, increasing volunteer numbers, improving employee morale, and growing the mission's community status.

All in all, doing good can come with a good number of challenges. But if you believe you're headed in the right direction, don't let a few distractions take you off course. The path you blaze could bring so many more good things to light.

CHAPTER 13

Segmenting, Targeting, and Positioning: Stop the LDG, Start to STP

Lunch, Dinner, and Golf (LDG)

In addition to lunch, dinner, and golf, add to the list "sponsorship" (of a child, runner, walker, or biker), and I've probably covered the anemic "strategic underpinnings" of most nonprofit marketing plans! The biggest problem is that these elements are really tactics (not strategies), and they don't help to differentiate your organization. As a matter of fact, they cause your organization to look like just another "face in the crowd" of nonprofits that rely on gimmicks or guilt to raise support instead of providing compelling and lasting reasons to give and give often.

To make matters worse, nonprofits that become reliant on such "fun-raising" efforts often experience declining returns over time or increased and unhealthy dependence on them (like a caffeine addict needing their recurring fix). The organization's credibility and true cause can so easily get neglected and ultimately lost.

Beyond all that, I find that many nonprofits using "L," "D," and "G" as the staples of their marketing and fundraising efforts often are not honest with themselves about the true costs of putting on these events. They'll say, "But this annual event raises thousands and thousands of dollars!" But they don't see that the hard costs, time, and effort required to stage the event make it difficult to provide a strong ROI and, in fact, the event may actually be a financial net loss!

I once worked with an international nonprofit that provided surgical healthcare for people in impoverished countries. They relied on a "celebrity" radio personality to host special donor weekends at exotic resorts. Besides being seemingly "off-brand" and contradictory—hosting people at a five-star resort to talk about poor people who can't get access to life-changing healthcare—they believed for years that these "weekends" were the reason their big donors gave to support the organization. The reality was, once they asked their donors if the weekends made a difference in their giving, they found that they did not! These donors had already made their minds up before these events how much they would give to this cause. So the events, for the donors, simply provided a nice social gathering with like-minded people and a chance to connect with the leadership of this organization.

Now add the time, energy, effort, and attention to the actual hard costs of this event, and this "fun-raising" event was quite costly and generated no additional funding. Nor was it an effective tool to expand their list of supporters.

Don't get me wrong: I'm not saying celebratory events and fun activities shouldn't be done with or for your donor base. Building stronger bonds and having low-risk ways for new donors to get to know your organization are both great ideas. But please don't try to turn a cost into a profitable venture.

Another common mistake made with LDG events is that, maybe at one time, they were effective in acquiring new donors and growing donations, but they fail to acknowledge that they've lost momentum and positive ROI since. I hear from nonprofits frequently that "one time" we had this event, and it was magical. Incredible contacts were made and donations poured in. And it's likely that "one time" all the stars aligned, and the event had its day. But that's no reason to perpetuate it and turn it into an annual ritual that loses money and costs significant time and energy.

My staff and my family can tell you I often repeat the definition of insanity (frequently attributed to Einstein) when seeing such patterns of behavior:

"Insanity is doing the same thing over and over and expecting different results."[12]

In the physical fitness world, we've all heard that the same exercises, done the same way repeatedly, have diminishing returns. Experts in that field suggest that your workouts need to include "muscle confusion," or what I would call "muscle variety." Marketing often works the same way. You do things that work, but you need to find new and fresh ways to exercise them.

Which Brings Us to the "STP Concept"

First of all, STP is not a fuel additive; it's an acronym for "Segmenting, Targeting, and Positioning." It's also not a tactics-based approach to marketing as LDG is. It's highly strategic and can help revive old tactics and create new ideas that add innovation, diversity, and excitement to your marketing mix.

The STP Concept summarizes and simplifies the process of identifying audiences, markets, strategies, tactics, and messaging. The STP Concept is generally chronological, although once strong strategies and targets are established, your positioning may change relative to competitive forces and messaging.

Here's how it works:

- **Segmentation** identifies the market to be segmented, divides your constituents by characteristics and tendencies, and then develops their profiles according to a range of variables.

- **Targeting** identifies the most attractive segments from the segmentation analysis on which to focus your attention. Usually the ones with the highest ROI are seen as primary while others are put into categories of secondary and tertiary.
- **Positioning** is the last step in the process, and it is the more message-oriented stage, where an organization assesses its competitive advantage or unique selling proposition (USP) and positions itself in the audiences' minds to be *the most* desirable option within their respective categories.

From this STP analysis, your organization's tactics can be reviewed, renewed, and developed to reach and influence the various audience segments. If you begin with the audiences you've identified as your primary ones first, it's usually a good idea (and wise stewardship) not to move on to other audiences (such as secondary and tertiary constituents) until you've maxed out all opportunities to grow and gain market share with your primary audiences.

So it's likely time to start thinking differently. Instead of revolving your marketing plans around tired LDG tactics, focus your energy on a different strategy: the STP Concept (Segmenting, Targeting, and Positioning).

In the next few chapters, we'll unpack these steps and see how you can start using STP to grow your impact and results. We'll start with segmenting.

CHAPTER 14

Audience Segmentation: The Best Direction Is Often a *Different* Direction

There's an Old Saying That Good Intentions Don't Move Mountains, Bulldozers Do

One mountain-moving bulldozer strategy that your nonprofit can benefit from is "segmentation"—dividing your audience into groups according to particular criteria. The members of each group have at least one important factor in common with the other members of the same group, and that factor sets them apart from all the other groups.

The criteria that you use to determine your groups should have some relationship to how they will respond to your message. Segmenting will help determine how you deliver your message, as well as its content.

By segmenting your audience, you'll be able to see them as distinct groups with different interests and needs, rather than one monolithic unit (which may or may not have the time or interest to do "lunch, dinner, or golf" with you!).

Here are some of the ways you can segment your support audiences:

- **Size of gift:** Small (under $100), Medium (over $100), Large ($1,000 or more), or Major ($10,000+)
- **Frequency of giving:** One-Time, Monthly, or Annual
- **Age:** Young (under 25), Pre-Mid (26–39), Mid (40–55), or Senior (55+)
- **Nest:** Young (no kids); Full Nest A, B & C (kids under 6, kids 6–13, kids 14+); or Empty 1 and 2 (no kids at home/still working and no kids at home/retired)
- **Reasons for giving:** Habit (always have/tradition), Self-Esteem (feels good), Belief (believe in mission), or Nuisance (looking to stop the ask)
- **Interests:** Faith (association with church or religion), Political (empathy with political leanings), Community (likes improving the community), Personal (impacted by the issue or cause), or Connection (knows someone who is/has been impacted by the cause or issue)
- **Behavior:** Active (likes to do things), Intellectual (likes to discuss things), Spectator (likes to watch others do or discuss things), or Generous (likes to help others do things)
- **Stage:** Beginners (new supporters), Movers (2–4 years of support), Builders (5+ years of support), or Lifers (multi-generational giving families)

I could create list after list of segmentation models for nonprofits to consider. What's important, though, is that your organization begins to segment its audience and starts to understand these different groups. This allows you to prioritize and serve their interests and needs in unique and compelling ways. Segmentation makes a huge difference in the messaging you use to communicate with these different audiences.

The key is to take the time to get insights into these various segments by talking with donors and volunteers who fit these profiles. While your overall messaging and brand promise should not change, how you communicate or provide experiences to connect with your brand should be crafted and shaped to fit these varied audience profiles.

You'll find that some donors or volunteers need facts to feel motivated and compelled to provide support, while others want hands-on or firsthand experiences to develop deep connections to your organization. Yet others may just be generous people who simply want to be reminded of your impact, thanked for their previous giving, and provided an easy way to support your mission again.

Divide and Conquer

By dividing your existing support audiences into various categories, you may find common traits among your most loyal supporters. Knowing that information will help your organization develop "look-alike targets" for acquisition of new donors (which, with the audience data available in social and digital media today, can be very rich and fruitful information to know).

I have worked with many nonprofits to segment their existing support base and have been able to help them narrow their targets and decrease their acquisition costs significantly. For one private nonprofit college offering a unique specialty degree program, for instance, we were able to lower their acquisition spend from a shotgun, national campaign effort to one focused on homeschool and Christian school families in the Midwest. We prioritized the segments in their audience by understanding exactly who provided the best ROI. At another private nonprofit college, which had experienced success by communicating its story on a specific radio program, we helped the college reinvigorate a development effort that had plateaued by digging in and understanding the audiences responding to those messages. Then we were able to leverage that information to find other media channels that could effectively communicate the message—and it worked!

I hope these examples help to get some ideas flowing and encourage you to begin thinking about ways you might segment your audiences to help differentiate your brand and maximize your efforts.

Next we'll focus on "targeting," the second step in the "STP Concept."

CHAPTER 15

Strategic Targeting: Setting Your Sights on the (Right) Targets

"Ready, Aim, Fire" vs. "Ready, Fire, Aim"

Taking the time to understand your target audiences and their needs is one of the most important things any organization can do. When you try to deploy "tactics" before putting energy into segmentation and targeting strategies, then *impatience* is really driving your development approach!

And that impatience can lead not only to "fire before aim" methods but also to "fire, fire, fire" programs that usually result in inefficiency and poor stewardship. You can waste a lot of money with "shotgun" methods. If you're aiming at everyone, chances are you'll hit no one.

Even worse are marketing efforts mired in *inertia*—"ready, ready, ready" program planning that fails to seize opportunities or does nothing because of fear.

Targeting, the second step in the STP Concept, is about setting your organization's sights on specific audiences, interests, and needs—and then choosing the strategies, messaging, and tactics that will best communicate with those particular constituencies. It's not a one-size-fits-all approach!

The American Cancer Society Gets Focused and Finds a Cure

A classic case of targeting was outlined in Philip Kotler and Alan Andreasen's book *Strategic Marketing for Nonprofit Organizations*, which documents successful outcomes that the American Cancer Society experienced when it became a target audience-driven organization.

In the 1990s, because of competitive pressures from other cancer-type causes, the American Cancer Society experienced significant decreases in its donations. As a result, the organization's first move was to focus on a small number of target areas: the elimination of tobacco use, promoting early detection of breast cancer, and intensified efforts in school health programs. Targeting these three specific audiences and their varied interests, combined with a few other organizational changes, brought great results. The increased donations included the launch of a new program that began generating more than $300 million annually!

The way the American Cancer Society arrived at these targeted areas was not specifically documented in Kotler and Andreasen's book, but it appears to be a clear case of target segmentation, research, and analysis.

Here's How You Can Follow Suit

Once you've segmented your constituencies into various demographic and psychographic groups, ask the following questions as part of your planning process:

- Which is the "lowest hanging fruit" (usually your largest, most obvious audience segments), and how many audiences can your organization afford to go after right now?

- Where can these specific groups be found? And what communication tools are most effective for reaching them?
- What are their current perceptions of your organization as well as their particular interests and needs?
- How satisfied are they with your organization's brand promise, purpose, and success? (We'll talk more about these in upcoming chapters.)
- Why do these target audiences support/not support other "competitive" organizations like yours?

Remember that "competitive organizations" are those that offer the same or similar services as your organization or seek support from the same or similar donors. You may not view them as "competition" in the nonprofit world, but your constituents need to know how you're different from these other organizations.

Once you've done this kind of thinking and analysis for your lowest-hanging-fruit audiences and you've attempted, perfected, and achieved success, you can then move down the line to other audiences that share many similar attributes, perspectives, interests, needs, or concerns to create secondary and tertiary audience targets.

A New Target Audience Perspective Can Make all the Difference

My friend Ken Calwell's resume is very impressive. He was once the successful and experienced chief marketing officer at Domino's Pizza, then Wendy's, and then he became the president and CEO of Papa Murphy's Pizza. He then made a choice to become an even greater force for good as the chief marketing officer and senior vice president of innovation for Compassion International. Compassion International is a sixty-nine-year-old child relief and child development organization focused on holistically serving the physical, social, economic, and spiritual needs of more than two million children in poverty in twenty-seven different countries around the world. During his career, Ken has been widely recognized for his many accomplishments, including being named by *Advertising Age* as one of the "Top 100 Marketing Leaders of the Year" six times, winning a Gold Effie marketing communication award, and being inducted into Indiana University's Kelley School of Business Brand Leadership Hall of Fame.

I've always known Ken as "Mr. Innovation." I observed the magic in his work—he didn't force agencies and his team to come up with campaigns that were full of fluff...he helped the companies he worked for discovery truly innovative new products and services. This enabled his partner agencies to create messaging to support the substance of those innovations. When I asked him to speak at our DO MORE GOOD conference a few years ago, Calwell asked, "How can I best serve the DO MORE GOOD audience? What topic would you like me to speak on?"

I replied, "You're known as 'Mr. Innovation,' but now you're at Compassion International—which is a not-for-profit that has been doing the same 'child sponsorship' marketing model for decades. They are not known for breakthrough innovation. So what's 'Mr. Innovation' going to do to change that?"

"Mr. Innovation," of Course, Innovates

He said, "Yeah, that's what we are working on. However, we are not just creating an innovation team, we are creating an innovation culture. Let me share with you my process for doing that. When I first joined Compassion International, I asked everybody, 'So who are our target audiences—who are we communicating with? Who is the customer that we serve?'"

Calwell said, "I found myself longing for the focus I had in the business world, where we inspired and aligned our organization and all team members around knowing and serving our customer. Building a 'customer-centric' culture was a proven 'best practice' that

I had seen successfully transform the sales, profit, and market share growth at Domino's Pizza, Wendy's, and Pizza Hut. It's true that, technically, customers, franchisees, stockholders, and employees were all separate 'target audiences,' but if I stayed focused on pleasing the *customer*, then all these different audiences were happy—the employees, the franchisees, and the stockholders. And beyond their self-interests of wanting a successful organization, they and their families, at some point, will all be customers. Therefore, in the business world, all my efforts could be laser-focused on the customer, and when I did that, our sales went up and growth happened. We just had to know our customer, know their needs, and then focus all of the organization on innovatively serving those needs.

"So my challenge when I joined Compassion International was, how do we build a 'customer-centric' culture at Compassion International? Who is our customer? However, I was asking the wrong questions. Compassion International is a not-for-profit team focused on a mission to release children from poverty. The for-profit world in which I had grown up has customers. Customers who, when served well, reward you with their visits and their dollars. The better you serve the customer in the for-profit world, the higher your sales and profits. The relationship between the for-profit world and their customers is primarily transactional. However, Compassion International is different. Compassion International is a 'not-for-profit.' Our mission is not profit—our mission is to release children from poverty.

"Our goal is not transactional; our goal is relational. Our goal is to know, love, and connect those who share our mission with the churches and children around the world who need their help most. Since our goal as a not-for-profit was not transactional, it was wrong to refer to those we served as 'customers.' The question was, 'Who are we serving?' Since most of my business textbooks had been written for the 'for-profit' world, I pushed them aside and reached for my Bible. In Mark chapter 12 verse 28, Jesus Christ is asked: 'Of all the commandments, which is the most important?' 'The most important one,' answered Jesus, 'is this . . . Love the Lord your God with all your heart, and with all your soul and with all your mind and with all your strength. The second is this: Love your neighbor as yourself. There is no commandment greater than these.'

"'Love your *neighbor* as yourself.' Jesus's goal was never transactional . . . it was always relational. Jesus always wants a deeper relationship with us. As a not-for-profit with a mission to release children from poverty, that's our goal . . . a deeper relationship with the *neighbors* that we serve. In November 2019, we made the commitment never again to refer to those whom we serve as 'customers,' but only refer to them as 'neighbors.' Changing that one word 'customer' to 'neighbor' is now changing our culture in significant, meaningful ways.

"When issues arise now, we no longer start with the 'how' question: 'How are we going to address this issue?' Our first question now is the 'who' question: 'Who is the neighbor that we serve?' We are now investing more than ten times the amount of resources as before in learning *who* our neighbor is, *what* our neighbors want most, and very importantly, *why* they want what they want. Only then can we fully answer the who, what, and why questions for the neighbors that we serve. And guess what? Once you have fully answered these,

- *Who* your neighbor is
- *What* your neighbor wants most
- And *why* they want what they want

"I have found that the how part . . . the 'how you serve your neighbor' part, which is the innovation part, becomes simple. If you start with the 'how' question, it's the hardest part. However, if you start by answering the 'who, what, and why' questions, then answering the how question is the easiest part . . . it practically reveals itself.

"That is what I mean by being 'neighbor-centric,' and that is the first and most important step in creating an innovation culture."

Know, Love, and Serve Our Neighbors

"Here's the concept: Everybody is your neighbor. One neighbor has money to give. One neighbor has time to give. And one neighbor is in need—but at any given point, people could change places, so we need to look at these very different target audiences with one perspective. That means, at any given time, a neighbor might have time or money to give, or they might need something or someone. But the key idea and mindset is that our audiences all need to be treated kindly and lovingly as a 'neighbor.' A neighbor that must be known deeply, loved deeply, and served well."

The Compassion International team and leadership agreed, and they had just started working with that new "neighbor-centric" perspective when the COVID-19 pandemic hit. Compassion relies on large, live, in-person Christian concerts and events to attract donors and donations. Due to the COVID pandemic in 2020–2021, Compassion had to cancel over 60 percent of these live, in-person events to protect their supporter neighbors and the public. The immediate assumption was that their donations would decline drastically.

Ken continued, "How can we talk to our donors as good neighbors during a time like this? Compassion was challenged to think of the ways we could best support our donors and serve them as our neighbors. Compassion decided to do two things—first, telephone donors individually to ask them how they were doing during this difficult COVID pandemic time. And secondly, we wanted them to know that if this was a challenging time for them personally, then they have Compassion's support and understanding to stop giving for a while and take a break. It's okay for them to do that."

I asked Ken, "What happened?"

And Ken said, "Much to our surprise, donations went up. Many donors wanted to give more to support and make up for those who could not give during this challenging time. The innovative philosophy of being 'neighbor-centric' grew this nonprofit through a worldwide crisis by treating their donors with the same love and care and nurture that they had shown needy children for decades."

And the Moral of the Story Is . . .

When you treat your target audience as you would want to be treated, whether each person is a customer or a donor, such actions and motivations build trust, loyalty, and support.

Too many nonprofits treat donors as ATMs and their fundraising goals as more important than demonstrating goodness to go along with good works. Ken's "neighbor-centric" innovative approach brought clarity and mindful innovation to Compassion International's efforts to raise support by raising the bar on how *all* audiences should be treated.

Regardless of whether you're planning to conduct your own research about your target audiences, you should force yourself to mine the data about your target audiences that you already have or that others have gathered (via secondary research) to see if there are new and/or more effective ways and places to aim your marketing efforts for better results.

CHAPTER 16

Positioning and Differentiation: Positioning Your Way into the Minds and Hearts of Your Audience

Jockeying for Positioning

Positioning is all about the battle for supporters' time, minds, hearts—and yes, their wallets. I know that might sound a bit crass, but people tend to support causes and organizations that they connect with and find personally relevant. And more often than we'd like to believe, they usually support the ones that are the most present and persistent.

The purpose of positioning is to create an identity in the minds and hearts of your target audiences that not only differentiates your organization, but also assigns certain values or attributes that they can espouse. In the consumer world there many classic examples such as United Airlines's "Fly the friendly skies" and Prudential Insurance's "Get a piece of the rock." Strong positions like these, of service and stability, help to identify for your donors why your organization is distinct, effective, and deserving of their support. Experts have written many books on positioning, but most of the principles can be boiled down to three basic strategies:

1. **Build on your strengths**: What is your organization really, *really* good at (better than your competitors)? Examples: Holistic care? Program completion success? Saving lives?

2. **Zero in on a niche**: What are one or two things your organization does exceptionally well? Examples: Speedy care? Quality staff? Tending to the needs of specific people, groups, or neglected areas?

3. **Reframe the competition**: What do you offer or provide that the alternatives don't? For example, is your organization high touch or high tech? Does it offer easier access? Lower cost? Greater efficiency?

Segmentation | Targeting | Positioning

An interesting positioning project with which I was involved was related to a nonprofit media ministry's feature film. Even though it had great entertainment value, the film they were looking to release was created primarily as an outreach tool. The makers of this particular movie were looking not only to score at the box office to help fund their efforts, but also to bring attention to and prompt discussion about important topics and pressing concerns in which they were engaged.

While the movie had a strong faith-based element, the producers felt that the storyline was universal enough to reach broader audiences. Beyond its biblical underpinnings, the movie also took place in a remote rainforest jungle and highlighted an oft-studied tribe of unusually violent people. It was historical in nature and was action-packed too. But with limited marketing dollars, we needed to focus our efforts on four target segments even though we identified close to a dozen potential target audiences. So we created positioning messaging for each of these four audiences. Following is how we divided the segments, target audiences, and positioning for this movie:

SEGMENTS	TARGET AUDIENCES	POSITIONING / MESSAGING
Behavioral	Christian Moviegoers	Two different worlds collide, creating new hope
Spiritual	Evangelical Christians	A powerful story of forgiveness and reconcilation
Ideological	Political Conservatives	An exciting adventure — triumph over tragedy
Demographic	Senior Citizens	The story you thought you knew has another side

Note that the "product or service" (in this case, a movie) didn't change—all four segments and audiences sat down to watch the same movie.

But how this movie was presented and promoted to those audiences was markedly different. Netflix also does this by creating various trailers to show people based on their viewing habits.

We allowed each audience the opportunity to connect with the story in a way that was unique and relevant to them. When it launched, the movie landed in the national box office top ten! It also became one of the top-selling, faith-based DVDs for a major Hollywood studio.

Ultimately, the STP Concept (segmentation, target audiences, and positioning) helps an organization to do more good. But as you can see with our movie example, it also allows people to personally connect and engage with your cause and "feel really good" uniquely and individually about their involvement with your organization. Then they can better communicate with their circle of family and friends about *why* they support your organization—on a personal, emotional, and inspirational level.

Getting Really Personal (and Inspirational)

Another powerful insight-gathering tool is an exercise to help you examine your brand's personality and how it could change or be enhanced to better match with the position you want to own in your category.

When engaging in this exercise, you'll want to go beyond getting a read on the *current* state of your brand personality. You'll also want to decide whether it matches your *desired* personality.

You can pinpoint these insights in several ways, but here are five key questions to make this exploration easy and fun as you discover key positioning insights about your brand:

1. **If your brand were a famous person, who would it be— and why?** From my experience, this question tends to unlock great insights because it allows you to "personify" your brand (project a personality that paints a strong picture of your brand). You can get even richer insights when you ask/answer a few follow-up questions. What characteristics of that famous person are dominant traits of your brand? What traits might be considered "character flaws"?

2. **Now that you've defined your brand as [fill in the name of a famous person], is there another famous person you would like your brand to be instead? If so, who—and why?** Obviously, if you or your leadership group likes the current personality of your brand, you can skip this question. Frankly, though, I have not found an organization in all my years of using this material that didn't want to have a slightly different personality.

Before moving on to even more insightful follow-up questions, here are a few examples of how other organizations I've worked with have answered these questions. While the organization names are generic, the examples are real.

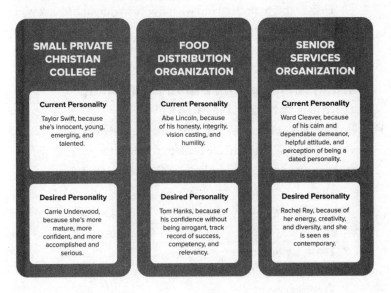

SMALL PRIVATE CHRISTIAN COLLEGE	FOOD DISTRIBUTION ORGANIZATION	SENIOR SERVICES ORGANIZATION
Current Personality Taylor Swift, because she's innocent, young, emerging, and talented.	**Current Personality** Abe Lincoln, because of his honesty, integrity, vision casting, and humility.	**Current Personality** Ward Cleaver, because of his calm and dependable demeanor, helpful attitude, and perception of being a dated personality.
Desired Personality Carrie Underwood, because she's more mature, more confident, and more accomplished and serious.	**Desired Personality** Tom Hanks, because of his confidence without being arrogant, track record of success, competency, and relevancy.	**Desired Personality** Rachel Ray, because of her energy, creativity, and diversity, and she is seen as contemporary.

Digging Deeper, Striking Insight Gold

Once you've determined who your brand is and who you might like it to be instead, dig deeper to uncover more golden insights:

3. **What is your brand personality's emotional appeal?**
   How does your organization make people feel? How would someone working with you benefit?

4. **What words best describe your organization's work?**
   What deliverables or services does your organization provide? What impact do you make on the people, community, or world around you? Who do you serve and get support from?

5. **What are you really good at doing?**
   What do you do that's the best of the best? What do you do that is clearly unique to your organization? What do you do that's much like the competition is doing? (Be honest

with this last question, but these probably aren't the attributes to highlight when describing your brand. You should answer this to understand what not to highlight because it's a commodity.)

Crafting An Insightful Brand-Positioning Statement for Your Nonprofit

To wrap up this exercise, look at the words you've used in each category and see if you can combine them into a short phrase (ideally, no more than nine words) to develop a memorable brand-positioning statement.

Here are a few "nine-words-or-fewer" Brand Positioning statements we've worked with:

- **Youth Camp**
  Equipping future leaders through fun, meaningful experiences.
- **Faith-based Legal Alliance**
  Defending people's rights to live out and express their faith.
- **Child Welfare Agency**
  Rescuing children from the cycle of abuse and neglect.

Author Simon Sinek says, "Communication is not about saying what we think. Communication is about ensuring others hear what we mean."[13] Positioning and personifying your brand give your intended audiences a clearer and fuller picture of what you're saying and how you mean to do more good.

How about your organization? Are you segmenting, targeting, and then positioning—or are you still relying on the hope-based strategies such as "lunch, dinner, and/or golf" to attract donors and make a difference for your cause? Also, are you projecting the right personality to attract the kind of support you need today? Or are you stuck with a dated personality that is neither relevant nor impactful?

CHAPTER 17

Laddering Exercise: Take Your Positioning Up a Rung—or Two or Four

My goal is to help you and your organization design strategies that get results and enable you to do even more good. Positioning leads to differentiation . . . differentiation leads to breaking out of the sea of sameness . . . and by garnering the awareness and attention your cause deserves, success will follow.

But success is never easy. I helped a friend of mine launch a nonprofit outdoor concert series to help fund various community efforts, and after a less-than-successful first concert, she wisely said to me, "Well, I've never heard anyone who has launched a successful venture say, 'Wow, that was easy!'" (We did achieve much greater success from the second concert of the series, in part from what we learned after the first concert!)

The same goes for successful positioning. More often than not, an organization needs to work hard at making their marketing and fundraising programs stand out and get noticed. Often it will take a few tries and many tweaks before you'll start tasting success. But that job is a lot harder if your organization's efforts don't start with a plan to differentiate and reach higher.

Reach Higher, Ladder Up!

Ask someone who works at or leads another nonprofit to tell you about their organization, and they'll likely give a generic response about the organization's basic function and purpose. For example, someone working for a rescue mission might say, "Our organization provides food and shelter for hundreds of people in our city." In branding terms, answers like this provide base-level attributes and are considered the lowest form of positioning. As a matter of fact, this really is just "information," and I'd be hard-pressed to put this type of answer into the category of "positioning" at all.

Given this typical response, I use a tool known as "laddering" to help nonprofits move away from base-level, informational answers, and toward inspiring others with their organization's inherent emotional benefits.

Here Are the Steps

Like climbing a ladder, it's always smart to start at the bottom rung and work your way up, which gives you perspective to create extraordinary brand positioning:

Rung 4. Higher-End Benefits
   Inspirational and emotional aspects
Rung 3. Mid-Level Benefits
   Meaning and aspiration
Rung 2. Low-Level Benefits
   Needs met, solutions provided, and wants satisfied
Rung 1. Base-Attributes
   Basic function and purpose

I often use the example of a client that demands more out of its donors than the average nonprofit: a community blood bank. In its situation, the organization needed more than people's time and money—it wanted people's *blood* too!

Here's how I worked with the board of directors to ladder this blood bank up to better positioning. Listed here is each step (in reverse order from the preceding list), along with the final statement we arrived at for each level of the process.

Rung 1. Basic function and purpose. This blood bank collects blood every day in a centrally located, state-of-the-art facility and provides it to area hospitals for people who really need it.

Rung 2. Needs met, solutions provided, and wants satisfied. We're a community blood bank As a result, the blood donated through us stays in our local community and will not be shipped outside our immediate area. (This is a point of difference between this organization and a larger, internationally known blood bank with a location nearby.)

Rung 3. Meaning and aspiration. When people need blood in our community, their situation is often dire. So we're really a lifeline for our community!

Rung 4. Inspirational and emotional aspects. Because of our work and the support of our donors . . . our organization helps to save at least one life in our county *every day!*

Admittedly, I'm squeamish about blood, so this ideation session was a little rough for me. (I nearly fainted on the facility tour.) But if I were told, "Because of our work and the support of our donors, we can together save a life in our county every single day," I'd certainly be more inclined to give my time, money, and even my blood. (The complimentary Krispy Kreme doughnuts for donating is a nice incentive as well!)

What do you think? Could your organization step up how it talks about its positioning? Would telling people the inspirational and emotional aspects of your organization first leave them wanting to learn and know more?

Try "laddering" as a tool to position your organization to do more good.

CHAPTER 18

Why Messaging: What, How, or Why?

Questions Determine Results

A few years ago, author Simon Sinek released a leadership book titled *Start with Why*.[14] His hope was to help people encourage others to do things that inspire them—and maybe even change the world. Sinek originally covered this topic in a TED Talk,[15] which has been viewed by millions of people on YouTube.

Sinek explains how this concept applies to organizations as well as individual leaders. He points out that leaders of successful organizations motivate their staff and supporters around the concept of "why"—a single purpose, cause, or belief that serves as a unifying, driving, and inspiring force.

Less effective organizations, from his observations, lead their organizations focused on either their "how" (actions) or worse, the "what" (results).

Sinek's message is that if you start with "why" (emotional, purpose-driven values and beliefs), people will notice there's something special about your organization. And anyone connected to it will enjoy satisfaction and success.

While Sinek's advice is aimed at for-profit companies, nonprofits should already do this naturally. Their causes could be rallying supporters to identify with them and get behind their causes—better than any business.

So why are nonprofits so bad at communicating their "why"?

Why do consumer and corporate messages often connect emotionally more successfully than do messages from nonprofits?

I know this answer is a little like Abbott and Costello's "Who's on First?" routine, but the answer is in their "why." Companies such as Nike, Apple, and Harley-Davidson have built a loyal following because what drives them has little to do with the "how" or the "what." Rather, these brands create a kinship and confidence in their products that's simply unduplicated by their competitors.

For example, Nike's "why" is built around its deep love of athletes and helping them perform better. Apple's "why" is built around its desire to challenge the status quo and unlock creativity. And Harley-Davidson's "why" is about being independent in a world of conformity.

Sadly, I'm hard-pressed to think of a nonprofit that connects emotionally as well as these brands! Some have tried, like the ASPCA with its sad animal ads or commercials about paying a dollar a day to feed a child. Unfortunately, examples like these can go overboard and turn off people to their causes.

I can cite many reasons why nonprofits fail to connect emotionally with audiences (e.g., money, frequency, research, or talent), but product makers usually need to "manufacture" an emotional connection for their followers. Nonprofits, on the other hand, already have an emotional "why" that's inherent and real. So why can't the voice of charity, human kindness, and common good compete better in the battle of emotions with the consumer market? Frankly, it's often because nonprofits just need to know how to communicate their "why" better.

Finding and Intentionally Communicating Your "Why"

How can your organization's messaging be framed to better connect emotionally with staff, volunteers, and supporters?

Here are five ways to help find and build on your "why":

1. Explore with your organization's key stakeholders the reasons why your organization does what it does.
2. Find a way to express this in simple, emotional terms.
3. Test a few statements with your supporters and staff to find the one that is the most compelling and motivating.
4. Ensure that leaders and staff members, even volunteers, embrace and personalize their "why" statement. They need to make it their own by building from their own experiences.
5. Create a culture built around your "why."

The ROI of "Why"

From Sinek to the current "B Corp movement" (businesses that seek to balance profit and purpose), a community of leaders is forming into a global movement of people using business as a force for good. You might say these "B Corp" organizations are a hybrid between for-profit and nonprofit.

In short, businesses have found there's good money to be made in being perceived as doing good. Younger consumers have identified their strong desire to be especially loyal to brands that they believe stand for something greater than profits. And they're willing to pay more to support these businesses, which helps ensure a company's profit margin.

Clearly, when the corporate world recognizes a trend that is good for the bottom line, they waste little time before investing significantly in efforts to maximize their success. Why? It's just good business.

For nonprofits, being good is vital to who they are, so it may seem redundant to constantly beat the drum to let their publics know why it matters. But taking a page from the business world, it does matter because communicating your "why" and expressing it well unlocks your organization's ability to do more good.

So what is your organization's "why"? Can you honestly say it's more emotive than Nike's, Apple's, or Harley-Davidson's? If not, keep pushing until it is, because I'm sure it's there if you're willing to invest the time and resources to find it.

CHAPTER 19

Message Testing: How "B" Became *Bad*

I've always been a creative person, but I'm a little unique in that I don't have just an advertising or communications degree—I also have a marketing degree. So I've always had a great appreciation for the really deep-thinking, analytical side of taking an idea or product to market.

This means I probably have more respect for research and strategy than the average creative-oriented professional. Through the years, I've worked for many big brands and seen the results of having tremendous research and insights into audiences through message and concept testing.

Knowing exactly what to say and testing concepts to discover what's most compelling and motivating for the intended audiences give one direction and confidence. I've always believed that message testing was important, but I really learned how powerful it can be when I was doing a lot of work on cause- and issue-related political campaigns. That's where I experienced what happens when you combine a powerful message-testing process with tracking and polling.

One of the political campaigns on which my firm was asked to work was in opposition to physician-assisted suicide in Michigan.

Oregon had become the first state to legalize physician-assisted suicide, and proponents wanted to bring it to a vote in Michigan next. At the time, Michigan was the epicenter of that issue, and if proponents could win here, their platform could conceivably sweep through the entire Midwest ... and across the nation.

One of the best-known proponents and practitioners of physician-assisted suicide was Dr. Jack Kevorkian, who lived in Michigan. Kevorkian's attorney was running for governor in Michigan, and this referendum question would be on the same ballot, so a lot was at stake, and the national media was paying attention.

The early polling was predicting the measure would pass by a large margin, and the initial language developed by the opponents to this issue was not moving either the people or polling numbers! So my firm was hired to help defeat this initiative when it came to a statewide ballot vote.

I met Gene Ulm during this campaign. Gene's a partner at Public Opinion Strategies in Washington, D.C. He introduced me to polling, tracking, and a concept known as "proposition research." His firm, Public Opinion Strategies, used this method, which involves holding focus groups, conducting surveys, contacting thousands of people to seek informed opinions, and identifying the key messages that resonated with voters to encourage them to vote against this ballot initiative. They worked to understand the precise language that people found compelling—how they prefer ideas to be expressed and how they would react to specific messages. Then they started organizing those answers into "buckets" (or categories) of content.

Focus Groups. Direct Questions.

Gene's firm asked people in the focus groups tough questions such as, "Should doctors actually be in the business of ending lives? What about the oath they've taken to always try to protect and save lives?"

Then they asked the focus group respondents questions about the motives of insurance companies. For example, "Do you think insurance companies might want people to die without extraordinary efforts so that they don't have to spend as much money on healthcare, especially for older people?"

From there, Gene's firm started writing propositions for the various messaging content "buckets." Those would hold propositions under headings such as "Violating Hippocratic Oath," "Insurance Company Pressure," and "Michigan Becoming Known as the Death State." Then they would call thousands of people on the phone to "test" various propositions within these buckets to find the best way to articulate a message and get the desired outcome. His firm asked respondents to judge "Message A" versus "Message B" to see which was more successful at moving the needle toward voting against this initiative.

From there, the researchers would literally hand our agency a list of the messages that they had tested and say, "These are the top fifteen propositions, in ranked order, that we need to communicate in the ad campaign to maximize success at the polls."

Fifteen Messaging Options and 65 Percent Awareness Triggers

The plan was to put only one ad into the market at a time, each one focused on a specific proposition. Every night, polling would be conducted to measure the public awareness of that message. Gene's firm would ask people, "Have you heard or seen an ad that said this?" Once the awareness response rate hit 65 percent of audience recognition on any given night, the campaign was directed to immediately start running a new ad featuring a different proposition from our list of fifteen options.

It Was Eye-Opening

This is one place where I see a lot of nonprofits get stuck because they fail to objectively see their organization, its mission, and its messaging as the public sees them. They don't perform the kind of research that's routinely done in political campaigns and for large consumer brands, with focus groups and polling, to understand the different ways that people think about and respond to their organization's messaging. They don't ask the important questions about how an audience's behavior or action will be enhanced or changed as a result of receiving a specific message.

As such, nonprofits get stuck in one way of saying things, one messaging style, just hoping that it resonates with their target audience. And then they spend money on the creative work around that message, simply believing that it will compel and motivate people to react. It's all guesswork! They aren't willing to invest money and time into testing different messages to understand what appeals most to their audiences. So they are really just throwing money at what they hope will work!

In short, many nonprofits fail to understand that when you increase your knowledge of the marketplace and how it responds to specific messaging, you decrease your risk. And because of the mindset not to spend mission funds on messaging research, they rely on hope. They hope that their messages will resonate. They hope that what they're saying will break through and cause someone to respond. They hope that what they're communicating differentiates their organization from other forces competing for people's limited and discretionary time and resources.

The problem is "hope" is not a very good strategy.

Message #5 Turned Out to Be #1

Ranking messages is an important exercise, but sometimes execution trumps strategy. That was certainly the case in this campaign where the fifth-highest ranking proposition turned out to be the driver for an ad that had the greatest impact on voting outcomes.

Does that mean our testing was inaccurate? No, it just means that sometimes the *way* you say something can be as important as *what* you say.

The ad that moved voters the most was titled "Death State." The messaging was clear and very precise. It told the story of how Michigan could become a "tourist destination" for people who wanted to commit suicide if this proposal passed. It was a television ad that was filmed in a beautiful Irish Catholic church graveyard, and the ad started with an announcer saying, "Throughout history, people have wondered, where do we go when we die." The camera moves through the graveyard and ends on a gravestone in the "mitten" shape of Michigan, as the announcer continues: "If Proposal B passes and physician-assisted suicide is legalized in our state, the place people will go to die could soon become…Michigan. Proposal B is *bad* for Michigan!"

That campaign started on September 1 with the election and ballot measure scheduled for a vote in early November. As soon as the ads started running, we saw an immediate spike in the numbers trending in our favor. That spike continued until election day—when every single county and every single demographic in Michigan voted against the referendum—ultimately barring physician-assisted suicide from being legalized in Michigan.

When we first polled people in Michigan on this issue, 70 percent had said they were in favor of physician-assisted suicide and 30 percent were against it. After our campaign ended on election day, legalizing physician-assisted suicide was turned down by voters by a margin against of 71 percent, leaving only 29 percent in favor.

Take a look at this graph to see exactly how impactful messaging can be. Public opinion numbers were completely reversed in less than six months. A Pulitzer Prize-winning, nationally syndicated columnist called the effort "One of the greatest turnarounds in referendum history."

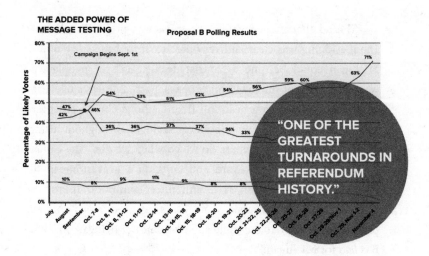

Yes, we executed some very compelling ads, but the reason this campaign was so successful was because of message testing, polling, and tracking.

It is important to understand from this example that you have the power in message testing to learn what you should say and focus on what works rather than wasting time and money by "guessing" and "hoping."

While it's a tough topic, and it can be tempting to politicize it, I use the Proposal B example to show you how nonprofits can think through and test their potential marketing messages, how they can work to perfect their language, and how they can then rank their messages to gain direction, confidence, and success. It's also important to stay disciplined and tell yourself, "We won't move off our top-scoring message until we've reached significant enough awareness of that message," which will help you focus your efforts and be good stewards of your resources.

How Long Can One Key Message Last? Just Ask GEICO

"Fifteen minutes could save you 15 percent or more on car insurance," says GEICO's gecko mascot. That message has worked extremely well for that company since 1999. They've found a variety of creative ways to portray it, but it's always been the same message. GEICO's commercials have won numerous awards, including being named the *Ad Age* "Campaign of the Year,"[16] and it has also earned the coveted Film Grand Prix award at the Cannes Lions International Festival of Creativity.[17]

Over the last twenty years, GEICO has also used that slogan to help it become one of the largest insurance companies in the United States.

Message testing is a great tool to help your organization find a strong platform that works well with your target audiences. And when you find a message that works, you might as well stick with it. Like GEICO, you can always find new ways to express your key proposition, but you don't need to switch to a new message because you might be tired of it. If it works…it works! Objective message testing will let you know how well your public recognizes and responds to your message, and if it's not working, then you'll know it's time to test some new "proposition buckets" to find out how to evolve your messaging.

Put It to the Test

It took me years to appreciate this testing process. I used to think, *We can just create creative ads that we like and our clients like. We don't need the research companies to tell us what to say.* Fortunately, I once had a really wise client; she listened to me bellyache about how I thought messaging research and testing were unnecessary expenses. I vividly remember one phone call where this client listened to me, and she didn't say anything. Then, when I finally stopped whining, she very politely said, "Bill, I want you to know that I hired a research firm to do research and messaging strategy. I hired you to create ads based on what they discover. And that's how we're going to do it. In other words, stay in your own lane!"

Today it's easier than ever for an organization like yours to do its own survey once you see the need for it. Online survey tools make it easy to set up questionnaires and make it even easier for people to respond. Incentivizing people with a gift card or drawing to win a prize also helps motivate people to respond.

The beauty of this kind of message testing is that it's science and art working perfectly together and valuing what each one brings to the table. Those research guys in Washington, D.C., with whom I worked on Proposal B now call me frequently and say, "You turn our research and messaging strategies into such artful expressions! We see how you help us to have a greater impact." So they get results, and they see the marriage of testing and creative is, indeed, a beautiful thing.

The Objective Truth and Nothing but the Objective Truth

Ultimately, there are and always will be many opinions within any organization about what kind of messaging works. What an organization really needs is not more opinions, but more *informed* opinions. Testing messages creates objective truth that truly helps an organization thrive.

It's so important to be disciplined and utilize messaging research to arm your organization with the lethal weapon of objective truth. To do that, you've got to go outside your organization and run some trial balloons with your messaging to see how people take it.

I learned from my Proposal B experience in Michigan that I can't rely on my opinion or my gut reaction, no matter how smart and creative I think it may be! I've got to hear what real people in the public are saying and whatever the market is relating to—that's what

I'm going to create my ads to say. I want to market messages that work with the results that can only come from testing.

That's what "Direction" is all about. Next we'll look at the creative and innovative aspects of "Expression" and see how that works for nonprofits.

PART IV

EXPRESSION

IDEAS PROCESS
E = Expression

I'm a believer in exploring ideas . . . a lot of ideas. Here's my current firm's tagline, partially because we're located on the shores of Lake Michigan: "Ideas in waves." That demonstrates how serious I am about creating many creative and story-telling options for my clients to consider.

I know from being in the idea-generation business for over thirty years that there have been many moments when a breakthrough idea came just as I was feeling I had exhausted all possible ideas. That happens far more frequently than when a great idea pops into my brain right away. Exploring lots of ideas usually pays big dividends.

Beyond the point of pushing yourself to always explore more, you need enough ideas to try on. Having options allows you to see which one "fits best" and is the most comfortable. Not many shoppers enjoy a store that has a limited selection. The same concept applies to shopping for the right brand fit; you should feel as if you have many good options to consider and that your final choice is just right for your organizational style.

How you express your organization's brand needs to feel right, given your history and approach, your market, and targets. And it needs to be the right response to competitive forces.

Many communication people and agencies like to limit choices. They position themselves as the experts who should know best what you need and how your organization's brand should be expressed. Experts may offer their point of view, but it's ultimately the organization that needs to live in and with their brand—so it has to fit well.

Ultimately, communication people and outside agencies need to see themselves as *interpreters* of dreams and not *creators* of them. Good work can be done by an individual, but I've learned that *great* work is almost always expressed by a team.

CHAPTER 20

Persuasive Messaging: The Seven Triggers of Persuasion

Listening and Encouraging— Not Talking and Pressuring

Almost every marketing expert and article agree that the most motivating and convincing methods of persuasive marketing and messaging techniques are those that focus on the personal benefits for the donor giving to and supporting an organization or cause, rather than focusing on the needs or wants of the organization.

This idea contends that an "outside-in" messaging platform is always more persuasive than an "inside-out" platform. That's because people are usually motivated more by feeling as if they're an active part of the solution, instead of feeling like they're being pressured into doing something as a reaction to a need.

Having an outside-in approach to communication means you express aspects of your organization in terms of what your donors will get or receive if you are successful in your mission. An inside-out approach communicates what your organization gets or receives if they are supported by donations.

Bank Accounts Don't Donate Money ... People Do!

People don't give to organizations—they give to *missions*. And they give more frequently and consistently to missions that align with their personal values and perspectives. Beyond that, a key motivator for ongoing giving is when donors feel they're part of the success and not just a tool being used to achieve it.

That means anytime your messaging can be benefit-oriented, not just to the beneficiary but also to the donor, you're likely going to gain a more loyal donor than if you "guilt" them into giving.

So switch your messaging to include benefits that your donors and volunteers can receive when they support your organization or cause, instead of communicating just what the organization or beneficiaries will receive, and you're ready to use the following seven key persuasion "triggers" to grow your giving. Consider using these triggers when developing your "benefit-oriented" messaging for appeals and campaigns:

1. **Empowerment**—Make people feel they have more control or influence when they support you. Unions, political parties, and think tanks use this technique very effectively, convincing supporters that change will happen if we all work together. And their constituents feel empowered as a result.

   President Obama's "Hope and Change" messaging used in his inaugural campaign efforts empowered a diverse mix of voters to support his election. The famous "Rosie the Riveter: We Can Do It" poster messaging helped empower female workers to roll up their sleeves and get behind the defense department in World War II.

2. **Desire**—Focus on feelings rather than data to create a sense of momentum and urgency. Cancer and juvenile diabetes causes have long been able to engage supporters by the progress made and the urgent need to close in on a cure that

can help our families and friends. Real people, their battles and their victories, are typically the focus of their effective messaging—not scientists, doctors, or hospital buildings.

The Susan G. Komen for the Cure foundation creates desire (and support) as well as any nonprofit. Just google it and you'll see messaging such as "put an end to this disease" and "investing in breakthrough research to find a cure." All such messaging creates a clear desire to get involved and help make a difference.

3. **Achievement**—Being in a special or select group is always appealing. And being part of a select group of individuals who are known to encourage or create good is even more attractive. When you provide volunteers or donors with emblems that can be displayed or shared, especially in today's social media world, you give them a much-appreciated sense of belonging, fulfillment, and recognition.

Forbes Funds advances the well-being of critical nonprofits in the Pittsburgh area. They issue digital badges for learning certifications as well as participation and attendance at events. The badges come in silver and gold levels based on established and well-articulated measurement outcomes. And they make it easy to obtain, download, and share achievement badges.

4. **Urgency**—While you can only yell "FIRE" so many times, uniting people through legitimate crises and concerns is very persuasive. This typically means that you need to define the consequences of not taking action now. Obviously this is easier for appeals that are truly urgent (like during or after natural or man-made disasters), but matching grants and limited-time opportunities (such as properties that suddenly become available) are viable urgent concerns. Just be sure to avoid the temptation to focus your messaging on the immediate or short-term impact to your

cause or organization; instead, focus on the "lasting impact" your supporters can make by acting now.

5. **Disruption**—Call your audience to change something in their culture! People generally like to think of themselves as progressive and able to find alternative solutions to problems. Young people (really, anyone under sixty) find this type of messaging especially appealing. The younger your support audience is, the more likely they are to gravitate to a message that communicates your campaign as an act of "rebellion." Legal alliances as well as animal rights and environmental groups use disruption very effectively. And it's amazing how long many of them have been able to sustain the position that they are the "new" alternative—even decades beyond the point of becoming a fairly mainstream organization.

DoSomething.org has been successfully disruptive by matching young people with opportunities that do not require money, a car, or an adult—everything is done via mobile devices. And GivingTuesday.org, which unites the U.S. philanthropic community for a day of giving at the start of the holiday season, has created new giving opportunities and increased giving awareness significantly since its launch in 2012.

6. **Empathy**—By demonstrating through your communication that your organization has a greater understanding of and compassion for the people, animals, or things you intend to help, your supporters will be convinced that they can channel their concerns through you . . . because you care. Organizations focused on abuse and neglect of children, animals, or trees can be especially effective using this type of messaging. But using this approach means sharing insights and positive outcomes of those people, animals, or things that you and your supporters are seeking to impact.

Both PETA (People for the Ethical Treatment of Animals) and the Truth Campaign, which communicates facts around smoking and vaping, are great examples of "disruptive" nonprofit messaging. Behind the extreme visuals, use of celebrities, and publicity stunts are lots of powerful messaging that make you empathize, in a visceral way, with their causes.

7. **Familiarity**—Being the most trustworthy, safe, and recognized organization in your category or within a certain geographic location or demographic has its benefits. But it also takes years and years of consistent presence and effort to reach that point. Reinforcing the fact that supporters can easily place their confidence in your cause is a messaging technique that helps to accelerate this process and provides a strategic advantage to your position. As I'll continue to emphasize, frequency wins. While being the most familiar may seem boring and obvious, it clearly works!

    While the American Red Cross, The Salvation Army, and the United Way don't always deploy the most powerful messaging, they do understand the power of frequency and familiarity as repetition breeds retention and repeat action. In short, they are known brands and many people give to these organizations out of habit or desire to be associated with a known entity that does good.

How about your organization? Which persuasion trigger seems right for you and your supporters? You can use more than one persuasion trigger for sure, but always look to be consistent in tone, look, and personality.

CHAPTER 21

Disconnected Messaging: Six Reasons Why Messages Don't Connect

Inward vs. Outward

There are many reasons why nonprofits fail to connect well with their supporters and produce content that engages them. An article by Ironpaper, a B2B agency, provides statistics related to that challenge, especially in today's digital age. One of their most insightful statistics is that 53 percent of nonprofit marketers say they feel challenged to produce "engaging content."[18]

We've already mentioned the marketing philosophy of being inside-out instead of outside-in. Being inside-out means that your marketing efforts tend to be organization-centered. Outside-in is the opposite—your messaging and marketing are centered on your target audience and their needs and benefits.

Here are six clues that will help you recognize if your organization has a less-than-effective, inside-out marketing and messaging philosophy:

1. **You see your organization's key messages as inherently desirable.** After all, who wouldn't want to help your organization and its cause? And you're probably right. But that assumes your target audience has no other choice when it comes to where they could spend their time, effort, and money. Plus, it presumes that they're not leading incredibly busy and media-saturated lives!

2. **You blame your lack of marketing and messaging success on your audiences' ignorance or lack of motivation.** "If they only understood our needs!" or "People today are just too busy [with unimportant distractions] to get involved in our important cause!" Those are the commonly held and often-expressed beliefs of many nonprofit communication executives. They're right! But is it really the responsibility of your audience to drive change? Or is it the duty of your organization's marketing team to inform and motivate people to be participants in change?

3. **You put little or no effort into target audience research.** Audience understanding and motivation are issues that truly need to be known and addressed. How can you devise strategies and methods to accomplish these issues without talking to your target audience members (especially those who have not yet responded)? You may be surprised that even a little bit of insight or informal research can go a long way to correct big problems in your messaging and marketing.

4. **You only use marketing to promote your organization and its needs.** One-way conversations are no fun at all. Good nonprofit marketers instinctively know that the key to marketing effectiveness is building relationships with target

audiences. Given that, instead of the stereotypical, "Enough about me...what do you think about me?" approach to one-way nonprofit communications, why not start a two-way conversation with your key constituencies? In other words, invite dialogue, interaction, and engagement— and see what happens!

5. **You have a "silver bullet" marketing strategy, using the same tactic again and again.** E-blast. E-blast. E-blast. Sponsorship. Sponsorship. Sponsorship. Same audience. Same audience. Same audience. Hmmm...many nonprofits keep pushing the same rock up the hill, wondering why their marketing ROI and retention are so dismal. Maybe it's because their marketing plans are dismal too!

6. **Your "competition" is ignored.** Every message, whether it's from another nonprofit or a corporation, competes with your messages. Let me repeat: *Every message* competes with *your* message. It's a busy world; you should get busy and consider who *all* your competitors really are, and then look at how you can make your messages more compelling than theirs.

Do these six considerations help you see your assumptions more objectively and help you to start formulating a different approach? Persuasion starts with logic and reason, but it's emotion that's the true motivator.

CU learn or CU later.

I was invited to speak on the campus of the University of Colorado (known by locals as CU), which was not unusual since I've been invited by many college professors to address and present marketing and branding concepts to their classes. This gathering was larger than normal; several marketing and communication clubs on campus and professors had invited students to a special evening event to hear me speak about nonprofit marketing.

Because I live in West Michigan, I most often speak to college classes and gatherings in this region of the country. But I have strong Colorado connections because I attended the University of Denver; worked for Batten, Barton, Durstine & Osborn (BBDO) in their Denver office; and I once had an office and many clients in that region.

So I can tell you from experience that Boulder, Colorado, and West Michigan are not only in separate regions of this country, they are actually worlds apart. Especially when it comes to politics, public issues, and religion.

My presentation began with a video to introduce the student audience to the kind of marketing I have done, and it included samples of my work for various conservative causes and ideas. Before the two-minute video ended, several students got up to leave. This wasn't a big concern as it was an overflowing event with 200-plus students in an auditorium that was meant for about 150.

I stopped my video before the end and called out to the students leaving to ask, "Quick question for those leaving: Are you walking out because you have an emergency or someplace you need to be, or are you leaving because you disagree with what my work stands for?"

One young man bravely replied, "I'm leaving because of your work samples. I disagree with the views expressed in your work 100 percent, and I'm not staying to be preached to."

I told him I appreciated his honesty, but I also said: "You can still leave if you choose to, no judgment from me. But if you do, and later in life we're on communication teams that are on opposite sides of an issue, I look forward to kicking your butt."

Obviously, this got his attention and most of the students let out an uncomfortable laugh.

While the responding student was still dead in his tracks and looking at me somewhat puzzled, I added, "Because what I'm teaching—and I'm teaching, not preaching—are valuable insights about how to communicate more effectively. And if you choose not to learn and grow in this area, I will continue to have an advantage over you and others who represent opposing views!

"However, if you choose to stay, I believe you'll be better for it. With this knowledge, you'll be a better competitor. And if you can communicate your side of the story as well as I can communicate mine, together, we raise the civility and quality of discourse, and the public is better served!"

He smiled, seemed to enjoy the challenge, and chose to sit back down.

After the presentation, he came up to me, told me he was glad he stayed, and that he looked forward to the day when we were opponents but both serving the public well. I agreed with him, and we gave each other a fist bump.

That's how I feel about the information shared in this and other chapters. My hope isn't that I help train like-minded people to think just like me. It's that I help all communicators be better at communicating so those who need help and those who want to give help are all better served.

CHAPTER 22

Messaging Balance: Persuade with Reason, Motivate with Emotion

Anumber of years ago I was invited to Washington, D.C., to receive several awards on behalf of my agency. The event was for an issue-based, political awards show that I'd never been to before, and my friends on Capitol Hill told me, "You've got to come. It's pretty cool. You'll meet all kinds of important people there."

While political communication awards are not the most prestigious, I thought, *I'll just go and pick up our awards, meet a few famous people, and learn a little more about successful political campaigns.*

When I got to the awards show, held in a massive, posh ballroom, I couldn't believe how many people were attending this event. I talked with a few of them during the networking hour and quickly got the idea that this was a politically charged crowd. I didn't tell anyone why I was there; I just wanted to be a spectator for the evening.

But at the table where I was seated, it seemed that everybody was of a very different political persuasion than I was. It didn't take me long to figure out that the whole ballroom was filled with people who were for the issue that my ads were against! This was primarily because it was happening during a post-presidential election year, and my friends from Capitol Hill neglected to tell me that this crowd might not fully appreciate my work because of who or what it was for!

As the program began and award after award was given out, I got more and more uncomfortable, saying to myself, *I'm really in the wrong place, and I should have learned more about this group before I agreed to come!*

Finally the organizers announced the category in which my agency won the three top awards for statewide ballot initiatives. When they put our work on the screen, the whole place broke out in boos!

By the time they played our third ad, you couldn't even hear the narration in the ads because the "boo-birds" drowned out the public address system.

At this point, with my face flushed, I looked down and thought, *I'm just going to quietly finish eating my dinner, and then get out of here as fast as I can.*

Hope and change.

The last award of the night was for the "Campaign Manager of the Year," and it went to the legendary David Axelrod. He walked up to accept his award, and the first thing out of his mouth was, "I just want to tell this audience, 'Shame on you!'"

He went on to say, "Those ballot initiative ads that just ran are brilliant! The fact that you guys can't separate yourselves from politics and be willing to learn from each other, that's shameful! Instead of booing, you should be inspired by ads like those. You should be saying, 'I've got to learn to do ads that are as good as those!'"

A hushed quiet fell on that huge ballroom, and Axelrod went on to give an eloquent speech about how his campaign for President Obama, centering on "Hope and Change," had set a new bar for excellence in political campaigns.

As the ceremony ended, I walked up to Axelrod and was able to get his attention for just a moment. I told him that I was the guy who'd created those ads that everybody booed, and I thanked him for what he said. He remarked, "Well, I meant it."

I said, "I know you led the nationwide campaign for President Obama. And I'm curious, how did you come up with the core messaging of your persuasive slogan, 'Hope and Change'?"

He responded, intrigued, "Why do you ask?"

"Well," I said, "I'm usually a three-word slogan messaging guy since I've found that groups of three help aid memory and recall. I thought it was interesting that you only used two words in that campaign instead of three. So I'm just wondering, how did you happen to choose those two?"

He looked down at my name tag and said, "Bill, those may be the two most researched words in the history of the world! We got to 'Hope and Change' because those were the words that tested best and worked. You're asking me why not three words? I'm a three-word slogan guy myself. But literally, we couldn't find a third word as strong as 'hope' and 'change.' So we just locked in on those two!"

When he told me that, he was dead serious. "The two most researched words in the history of the world," and I realized again how utterly important audience research can be in creating persuasive messaging that resonates with people emotionally. It can change people's minds and even influence their behavior. I was also reminded that no matter what my politics or perspectives are on issues, I should always be open-minded and able to take a step back to learn from other successful marketers how to create an impactful message—and then, test it well!

How the Mind and the Heart Work Together to Guide Choices

The French novelist Antoine de Saint-Exupéry once wrote, "If you want to build a ship, don't drum up people to gather wood and don't assign them work, but rather teach them to long for the endless immensity of the sea."[19] In short, while reason and logic play a role in winning people over, emotion is a more powerful motivator. And that's certainly true when you're trying to raise support for a nonprofit organization.

In study after study, market research on consumer decision-making shows a clear connection to both the mind and the heart when it comes to buying (or buying into) a product or a cause. While we need logical reasons for making decisions, logic alone will not motivate us to take action, nor is it likely to change our behavior. Instead we need to feel that taking the action or changing our pattern of behavior will lead to greater satisfaction on a personal level.

Generally the most effective marketing and branding efforts for products and services target the emotions tied to an audience member's personal values. Self-esteem, security, peace of mind, and enjoyment are some of the common motivators regularly tapped by for-profit marketers. Nonprofits, on the other hand, typically need to connect with personal values that are outside of their audiences' self-image—values such as caring for others, concern for future generations, preservation of natural resources, and making a difference in the world.

Our Emotions Are Growing

From the time of the ancient Greek philosophers, we've understood the importance of both mind and heart decision-making. Making an emotional connection is absolutely crucial for nonprofit organizations, as well as companies, to succeed in today's competitive marketplace.

With the number of choices continuing to increase, as well as the number of causes deserving time, money, attention, and passion, an emotional connection is often the key differentiator and influencer for a person deciding to engage with your organization . . . instead of with a competitor. Some studies even suggest that people who buy or support things today are influenced by emotions almost five times more often than they are by reason! The persuasiveness ratio of emotion to reason is 24:1.[20]

Beyond the immediate impact on decision-making, marketers' claims and benefits based on logical reasons tend to fade and even vanish over time, while the impact of emotional messaging tends to endure and grow. It "sticks" in audiences' minds!

Try to Be More Positive

Making your messaging more personally relevant for your audience is the key to creating an emotional connection. Keep your messaging in a positive tone—avoid playing on emotions such as guilt or fear, putting people at risk, irresponsibility, or demonizing the opposition. A positive tone will go far to encourage your audience to respond favorably (so they feel empowered as difference-makers), and it will encourage them to respond more frequently (with increasing loyalty and retention).

How about your organization? Does your messaging have an emotional connection? If it does connect on an emotional level, is it positive, and does it foster both empowerment and loyalty? If not, please keep reading!

CHAPTER 23

Meaningful Connections: Is Your Brand Meaningful?

What Does "Meaningful" Mean?

More than 300 global brands were recently ranked by the worldwide media giant Havas using its "Meaningful Brand Index." The results of this index show that the more a brand contributes to improving the well-being of individuals, communities, and the environment, the more meaningful it becomes.

According to Havas, only 20 percent of the ranked brands were considered to have a positive impact on our sense of well-being and quality of life. While 90 percent of consumers expect brands to provide content, more than half the content from brands is not meaningful to consumers. In fact, the study also said that most people wouldn't care if 77 percent of the brands on the list ceased to exist.[21]

So despite the billions of dollars spent by many of the world's largest brands, most of them have failed to connect with consumers in a meaningful way. As a result, in the eyes of consumers, most brands today are meaningless commodities.

According to the director of this study, brands that earn people's love, trust, devotion, and attachment benefit greatly in today's media-saturated world. Brands that want to break out of their "meaningless" positions will "have to focus on making a difference to people, communities, and society that endures, resonates, and multiplies."[22]

Move from what you offer ... to what you mean.

For years, I've helped clients move from simply talking about what they *offer* to communicating what their organization actually *means*.

Both by instinct and by training, I've always believed in the inherent benefits of becoming more meaningful in the marketplace. And I've learned that when nonprofits focus their messaging and marketing on *meaningfulness,* then support and volunteerism flourish.

I've also witnessed that as an organization becomes more meaningful to its constituents and community, its earned and social media coverage grows more frequent and positive, and even the quality of its board members improves.

As I read the Meaningful Brand Index study, I couldn't help but wonder how nonprofit organizations would fare in a similar study. Would people care if 77 percent of them disappeared tomorrow? Would they even notice? My hope is that nonprofits would fare much better. But my sense is that they probably wouldn't, that they would do even worse.

Figuring Out What You Mean

There are several ways to determine whether your organization is meaningful. One method is to compare your organization's meaningfulness to your direct and indirect competitors (other organizations that provide similar services or speak to the same audiences for support).

A great tool for this comparison is mapping. Following is a mapping device that allows you to plot where you and your competitors stand in terms of meaningfulness using the core axis points of "Connection vs. Commodity" and "Important vs. Unimportant."

MAPPING MEANINGFUL CONNECTIONS

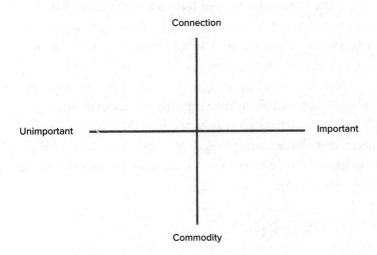

These definitions of the key mapping points help explain the axis points:

Connection vs. Commodity—a measure of the loyalty and passion of supporters by looking at things such as web traffic, social media engagement, and event/gathering attendance numbers.

Important vs. Unimportant—a measure of organizational awareness, understanding, consequence, and significance by the same measures offered in "Connection vs. Commodity" plus media coverage gained, prominent board or advisory board member involvement, donor counts, and funds raised.

Obviously, the ideal placement on this index chart is the far upper right corner, where high connection and importance meet and are maximized. You can identify and map your organization and its closest competitors using this Meaningful Connections Map. It may take a few attempts, some internal dialogue, research, fact-digging, external objectiveness (from those not employed by your organization), and honesty to chart everything. But it's a helpful and simple tool to assess how meaningful your organization is to your supporters. It may also tell you that your organization has some work to do when it comes to being more meaningful. Or that you have work to do to be more connected or more important than your direct and indirect competitors.

I love what Peter Drucker said: "Fund development is creating a constituency which supports the organization because it *deserves* it."[23]

My guess is that you're currently getting the support, love, trust, devotion, and attachment you *deserve*. I'd also guess that you believe your organization deserves a better and more meaningful position in the marketplace!

CHAPTER 24

Brand Cornerstones: The Multiple Dimensions of Your Brand

A brand isn't just one dimensional—many attributes add up to make an organization unique. Together these dimensions work to shape the key attributes people come to associate with your brand.

One tool I like to use to express these dimensions is the "Brand Cornerstones." These cornerstones represent the **four key perceptions** that an organization wants to reinforce and manage in the minds of those who engage with it.

Think of these dimensions as **decision filters.** They provide guidance and direction for reinforcing your brand in how you think and act, as well as in what you say, write, tweet, and post on social media.

Brand Cornerstones can represent the character you exhibit, the role you play, the services you provide, how you want others to feel when they engage with you, and the kinds of benefits they can expect your organization to deliver.

An organization can use its Brand Cornerstones not only to create outbound messaging, but also to train internal audiences how to reinforce these perceptions in all they say and do. The ideal result is that people will automatically associate these attributes with your organization—and believe them to be true.

At the center of these cornerstones is a Brand Promise, which we'll dig into deeper in the next chapter. Building the Brand Cornerstones is the foundation that will ultimately ladder up to an overarching Brand Promise—a logical, natural conclusion once the Cornerstones are established.

Laying the First Cornerstone—Your Reputation

Depending on the nature of your organization, this first Brand Cornerstone of "Reputation" can vary in the attributes it covers. For older, established organizations, this first Cornerstone may cover the "Heritage" of the organization. For organizations that are part of something bigger or an ingredient brand (an organization that supplies services to other nonprofits so they perform their services better or more effectively), this Cornerstone can be aptly labeled "Role." More often than not, I use the label "Reputation" for this Cornerstone as it is a good catch-all attribute that allows the history and/or role of your organization to be described.

The Second Cornerstone Is the Service Dimension

This one tends to be the most straightforward of the four Cornerstones, but it is amazing to me how often nonprofits can make this dimension more complicated than it needs to be. I often use Apple and Nike as examples of this "Service" Cornerstone, as they are tremendously complicated organizations with a wide spectrum of products, processes, technology, delivery systems, people, and locations. Yet these companies easily define themselves in the market daily. Apple makes phones and computers. Nike makes sports apparel, equipment, and accessories. Do they make and do more things? Absolutely. But everything they make or provide revolves around these core products and services.

So the inability of much smaller organizations to encapsulate their core product or service into a simple statement is often mindboggling and frustrating. Nonetheless, this "Service" dimension needs to communicate and communicate well to be a strong Cornerstone.

The Third Cornerstone Is Often the Most Important—Experience

In a few more chapters, we'll look more closely at "Experience" and how important it is to be influencing and creating successful outcomes. Ultimately, if you can't deliver consistently on a Brand Promise, then the Brand Experience you offer becomes a big question mark.

In the development of your Brand Cornerstones, it's important to think about how you want all constituents to *feel* about your brand and the impact you make.

It may be best to read the chapter on "Brand Experience" before trying to develop this particular Cornerstone for your own organization.

The Fourth Cornerstone Is Benefits

This Cornerstone can be complicated because your donors, staff, volunteers, and recipients all see those "Benefits" in unique ways. And it's likely that they all experience the various Benefits you provide differently. What are their takeaways when engaging with your organization? Some audiences experience Benefits directly while others indirectly. So the key is to articulate an overarching, higher order benefit that all your constituents enjoy or enjoy helping you achieve and that they clearly can associate with your organization. And make your Benefits emotional.

In the business world, Harley-Davidson has one of the simplest and smartest emotional benefits. You don't really hear them talk about it much, but it is an undercurrent that creates a lot of momentum. The emotional benefit a Harley provides, as they define it, is "freedom."

Harley-Davidson and its franchisees understand there are many motorcycle brands and even more apparel and accessories options on the market. Yet no other brand delivers the freedom you experience by being identified as a Harley rider and/or sporting the apparel.

What freedom do you get with the Harley-Davidson brand that no other motorcycle brand can deliver? The freedom to be the badass you once were—or wished you were. And the opportunity to display that attitude proudly on any weekend and in every town bar and on every street you roam.

Sounds like a lot of fun to some people. But the reality is, it's totally manufactured.

Knowing that, I constantly challenge nonprofits to express an emotional benefit for their organizations based on the real, heroic work that their staff, volunteers, and donors deliver every day.

Sure, Harley riders can look tough and cool. But my instinct tells me that the kind of work you do, expressed well, can move a lot more people and good things forward!

Following is a template to use to develop your own brand Cornerstones, as well as some samples of Cornerstones I've worked on for nonprofits of all sizes. Again, you may want to wait to finish this exercise after reading the next few chapters on developing your Brand Promise and understanding the important elements of your Brand Experience.

BRAND CORNERSTONES

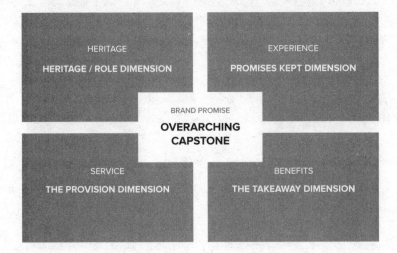

Career Skills Educational Institution

BRAND CORNERSTONES

Summer Camp
BRAND CORNERSTONES

HERITAGE
Who Is Summer Camp?
LIFE-GIVING LEADERS
Guides by your side sharing the Father's love
and wisdom at camp and beyond.

EXPERIENCE
How does Summer Camp deliver?
WONDER-FILLED WELCOME
Inviting campers to explore the wonder, peace,
and beauty of the Heart of God.

BRAND PROMISE
BEAUTIFUL BELONGING

SERVICE
What does Summer Camp deliver?
CONNECTED COMMUNITY
Developing deeper, lasting connections and a
strong sense of belonging in the family of Christ.

BENEFITS
What do Summer Camp audiences receive?
INSPIRED IMPACT
Investing in transformational growth that changes
lives forever and impacts future generations.

Faith-Based Organization Helping Jail Inmates
BRAND CORNERSTONES

HERITAGE
REDEEMING COMPASSION
Chaplains and volunteers provide a listening ear,
a loving heart, and a connection to Christ.

EXPERIENCE
REMOVING BARRIERS
Inmates can grow in their faith and learn how to
break free from destructive habits and patterns.

BRAND PROMISE
RELEASING LIVES TO CHRIST

SERVICE
RENEWING HOPE
Inmates receive compassionate care, the
opportunity to know God, and the ability to find
a new path forward in their lives.

BENEFITS
RECOVERING RELATIONSHIPS
Investing in transformational growth that changes
lives forever and impacts future generations.

Faith-Based Nonprofit Media Organization

BRAND CORNERSTONES

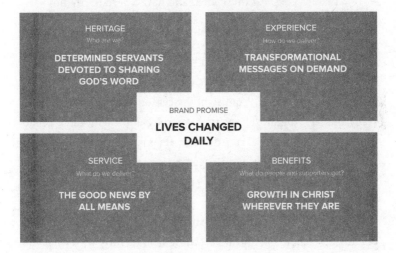

HERITAGE
Who are we?

DETERMINED SERVANTS
DEVOTED TO SHARING
GOD'S WORD

EXPERIENCE
How do we deliver?

TRANSFORMATIONAL
MESSAGES ON DEMAND

BRAND PROMISE
**LIVES CHANGED
DAILY**

SERVICE
What do we deliver?

THE GOOD NEWS BY
ALL MEANS

BENEFITS
What do people and supporters get?

GROWTH IN CHRIST
WHEREVER THEY ARE

Cornerstone Construction Tips

Here are a few things to keep in mind while you're developing your organization's Brand Cornerstones:

- **Alliteration**—Words that flow together the the ability to because they start with the same letter make it easier to remember your Brand Cornerstones.
- **Themes**—Ideas for wording that build on a common theme such as strong, wide, far-reaching, deep, lasting, and fast also have a memorability factor that is very effective and user-friendly.
- **Connections**—Brand Cornerstones built on connections to the environment, audience demographics, international scope, or meeting community-based needs also provide a memorability rhythm and heighten their meaning and importance for your audiences.
- **Ideas before words**—When you're working through the Brand Cornerstones in ideation, don't put immediate

pressure on yourself to find the right words. Instead, find
the right ideas or expressions and then work to find words
that best express those ideas and have a certain rhythm
to them.

The Capstone Is the Brand Promise

Having a strong Brand Promise in the center of these Cornerstones
really matters. Organizations with a strong and memorable Brand
Promise have more loyal constituents, allies, and supporters. People
place a higher value on your organization, your services, and the
impact you have when they clearly understand and align themselves
with your values.

In the sea of nonprofits, a strong Brand Promise helps your
organization stand out and attract those who identify with what you
believe and want to accomplish. It calls people to join you to positively impact the world or the world around them—and lets them
know what they can expect from you along the way.

Delivering upon your Brand Promise, not just giving it lip
service, is more than half the battle in providing a memorable and
compelling Brand Experience.

Inside, Outside, Onboarding, Off the Charts

The key aspect to remember about developing your Brand Promise
and Brand Cornerstones is that the wording used is meant to be strategic language. Which means they are meant to train, educate, and
motivate your internal audiences.

While many organizations I've worked with end up displaying
their Brand Cornerstones prominently in their office environments,
brochures, presentations, and on their websites, their core purpose
is to get everyone who represents your organization rowing in the
same direction by using common language, delivery standards,

and themes to express your brand consistently and well to the outside world.

An example of a globally known organization that has a strong set of Brand Cornerstones is Nike (though they only use three key attributes to support their Brand Promise). You'll rarely, if ever, hear their Brand Cornerstones expressed, but Nike's Brand Triangle is "Authentic, Athletic, Performance." That means everything they bring to market has to be authentically theirs with unique features and/or be designs that only they own. Everything they make is for athletes, and their products help athletes to perform better!

Internally at Nike, you'll see their "Brand Promise" hanging on banners displayed in almost every facility they run or own. You're probably thinking that their Brand Promise is the well-known phrase "Just Do It." But it's not; that's their tagline for external audiences.

Nike's extremely strategic and motivating internal Brand Promise is: "There Is No Finish Line," which speaks to the quality, innovation, and continuous improvement that has made them a global leader in their category.

Few if any of the words and work you put into your Brand Cornerstones are likely to end up being used as advertising copy or a tagline, but they will help you create those elements when it's time to do so. And more important, developing your Brand Cornerstones will help you deliver on your promises. You will have a strategic and competitive advantage with tools such as these that can take your nonprofit organization to new heights in success and impact.

CHAPTER 25

Brand Promise: Cross Your Heart

What's Your Brand Promise? And How Well Do You Deliver on It?

A Brand Promise is one of eight key elements of a brand. The other key elements are Brand Personality, brand name, logo, visual identity, verbal identity, tagline, and Brand Experience. But of all these, the Brand Promise is really the linchpin that holds these separate components together.

EIGHT ELEMENTS OF A BRAND

A Brand Promise is an expectation that your organization wants to create for your supporters, volunteers, staff, beneficiaries, and other people you serve. While it should directly relate to your positioning—which I unpacked in earlier chapters—it is a slightly different animal. A Brand Promise should be a concise statement of the outcomes or benefits you aim to deliver.

Some experts have referred to positioning as fertile ground that enables brands to grow, while a Brand Promise is the fruit. A Brand Promise can be clearly expressed in an organization's marketing efforts or, better yet, experienced by those who come in contact with a brand.

Some examples of Brand Promises include:

- **McDonald's:** An inexpensive, consistent meal delivered quickly in a clean environment.
- **FedEx:** Your package will get there overnight. Guaranteed.
- **Apple:** Providing power to people to innovate and create.
- **The Nature Conservancy**: Empowering you to save the wilderness.
- **American Red Cross**: Keeping lives together in times of crisis.
- **World Wildlife Fund**: Leading the most ambitious conservation effort the world has ever seen.

Do these promises line up with your perceptions of, or experiences with, these brands? If so, they're doing a great job of delivering on their promises.

Nothing without Delivery

A Brand Promise can help differentiate an organization in a crowded marketplace. However, if an organization doesn't consistently deliver on the expectations it created, then it will likely see a decline in reputation and support.

The temptation then is to make no promises at all! But that mode of thinking, obviously, has its costs as well: less appeal, lower value, little differentiation, and likely, no leadership position.

The key to a strong Brand Promise—besides creating one in the first place—is an organization's ability to execute and operationalize against it. Meaning, if you do not have internal buy-in, understanding, and training on how best to deliver on your Brand Promise, your chances for success diminish substantially.

Shoot for the Moon

Many argue that President John F. Kennedy's declaration that we would land a man on the moon and return him safely to Earth by the end of the decade was the greatest Brand Promise ever. Sure, new technological breakthroughs and scientific prowess were necessary to complete the task, but the real beauty of his promise was it lifted the hopes, dreams, and pride of an entire country (and many generations to follow).

That's the power of a compelling Brand Promise: It not only motivates supporters to think more and more highly of your organization, but it also sets internal expectations on a course to deliver even higher standards.

How to Get There

Knowing the impact a Brand Promise can make, here are some tips on how to create a new or better Brand Promise for your organization:

- **Keep your audience in mind.** Express your Brand Promise in a way that is ownable by your key audiences. In short, think less about "we can" and more about "you can."
- **Make it motivating.** Don't limit yourself only to what you can do and accomplish in the near term; push your promise into new territory that allows you to continuously expand upon your capabilities and strengths.
- **Share it.** Before you go to broader audiences with your Brand Promise, share it with supporters, volunteers, and staff to get their feedback. Collaboration gives you important insights and gives stakeholders a feeling of ownership.

Take a Measured Approach

As mentioned, it's smart to get some feedback from various stakeholders before you "go to market" with your Brand Promise. With online survey tools, it's becoming easier to get real-time responses from stakeholders rather than spending a lot of time and energy in laborious focus groups.

I suggest you test your top five or ten Brand Promise options with board members, staff, volunteers, donors and, if it makes sense, even the people you serve. The key with any type of messaging or creative testing is that you should avoid asking people what they "like" or "don't like." That's because those measures are far too subjective to base your organizational success upon.

Instead, create a survey scoresheet and ask people to rate each Brand Promise on these four benchmarks:

1. **Clear**—Can people "get it" without further explanation? Does it communicate the desired position in the marketplace? Are the differentiators transparently clear?

2. **Unique**—Could another provider of the same or similar services say the same thing? Does it sound fresh? Does it create differentiated expectations between your organization and competitive alternatives? Is it something you can own?

3. **Compelling**—Is the Brand Promise motivating, appealing, fascinating, or important? Can it inspire your priority constituents to act or believe? Is it meaningfully different?

4. **Believable**—Is it credible coming from your organization? If you say it, will people take you seriously? Is it based in reality, yet still inspiring?

Your scoresheet should line up all your Brand Promise options and allow each one to be rated on a scale of one to five (with one being "low" and five being "high" against these benchmarks). I recommend that respondents not be allowed to total their scores as people tend to want their favorite to score highest. Keep everyone objective by not allowing them to compare final scores.

Note: Many times, the "high-scoring" Brand Promises are not those that are chosen as the final Brand Promise for the organization. Winning this survey doesn't guarantee organizational acceptance. The person who leads marketing or communications in your organization, along with advisors such as the executive director, the board, and the organization's attorney, should use surveys as *part* of the process of making an informed decision. Ultimately you need to choose what's best for your organization based on all the information, experience, and expertise you possess.

One Small Step for Man . . .

The concept of space when you're working on your Brand Promise is one of the most important things to think about. Creating space between you and your competitors takes your brand to new heights. Differentiating elevates your brand.

One of those "small steps" you can do for a giant leap forward is to define your organization's "EST." That's not an acronym! It's a concept birthed by McMillanDoolittle in Chicago to describe the core competitive advantage of an organization in terms of how it's better than any other similar organization at being or doing *something*. And it means finding a descriptive word for your organization that ends in the letters "est."[24]

McMillanDoolittle works with some of the biggest retailers in the world, even direct competitors, and they can do it because they force each of their clients to define their organization's "EST."

Biggest, Tallest, Fastest . . .

You can imagine the challenge of asking a behemoth as complicated as some of the world's largest retailers to whittle down their brand to *one* word that defines them. That sounds impossible, but McMillanDoolittle knows it helps their clients' brands launch ahead of their competitors' brands and clearly define what they stand for. And if they can do it, you can do it.[25]

You're probably wondering which "EST" some of these retailers chose; well, Walmart is "lowest" and Target is "coolest." With that in mind, they manage everything they possibly can in their branding and customer journey to reflect and reinforce that one, ownable EST.

You know, as you talk to people about Walmart, they are always reinforcing the concept that Walmart has the lowest prices. And when you walk around a Target store, you feel "coolest" in virtually every touchpoint from its graphics, its carrying bags, its check-out aisles, and its house brands. Being "coolest" in Target's category has become such an important driving factor that I was told that Target even examined the kind of floor cleaner Walmart uses in order *not* to use the same kind or scent, because they said, "We even want to *smell different* from Walmart . . . we want to smell . . . cooler!"

That's what it takes to be a leader: Look at every detail and aspect of the way you run your organization and measure it against the EST promise you want to own in the minds and hearts of your priority constituents.

When you start thinking about applying this concept to your organization, think about a word that defines your core brand promise—what you do better than any other organization in your category—that ends with the letters "est." When you find that word, it really helps simplify everything your organization does.

For instance, I recently worked with a nonprofit organization, and after we brainstormed for a while, we came up with their "EST" and it centered on being "Deepest . . . the deepest connection, deepest understanding, deepest knowledge and, as a result, the deepest transformation, which then creates the deepest good, deepest hope, deepest truth, deepest love, deepest certainty"—the list can go on!

You can see how powerful that concept is—"deepest" is a rich word that distinguishes them from their "competition." A word like that starts to drive their communication, it starts to differentiate them from their competitors, and it answers the key question of their donors, "Why should I support you instead of someone else?"

The "EST" concept is also a great place on which to build your Brand Cornerstones since it includes many different dimensions that add up to your Brand Promise.

Some common ESTs include:

- Biggest
- Fastest
- Healthiest
- Safest
- Kindest
- Truest
- Purest
- Strongest
- Friendliest
- Fullest
- Soonest
- Toughest
- Easiest
- Nearest
- Baddest

In short, as Horace Greeley might have said, if you want to find *brand* gold, "Go (w)EST."[26]

CHAPTER 26

Brand Personality: The Heart and Soul of Your Brand

A Good Brand Personality Helps to Do More Good

Yes, Brand Personality is one of seven key elements of a brand. And while I've described an organization's *Brand Promise* as the linchpin that holds these separate key elements together, *Brand Personality* is really the heart and soul of a brand.

Brand Personality can be defined various ways, but simply put, it's an organization's character. It's how the organization talks, thinks, behaves, and responds. It's what attracts or repels people. It's the aspects of your organization that go beyond physical appearances and are more easily identified as your personality traits.

In nonprofit marketing terms, it has long been accepted that people don't choose to support organizations based on their mission and purpose alone. Rather, they also choose to support organizations based on their symbolic value.

Brand Personalities that inspire trust, encourage loyalty, create connections, and foster bonds are those that are considered more desirable, distinguishable, and memorable.

Attractive Personalities Attract Supporters

People tend to be attracted to Brand Personalities that align with or enhance their own self-image. This is especially true today when so many organizations have similar or overlapping missions.

Many times, in the absence of a well-defined and intentionally executed organizational Brand Personality, supporters and potential supporters "fill in the gap" with their own perceptions. Through years of conducting market research, I've found that brands with weak or unidentifiable Brand Personalities are usually labeled with negative descriptors—people usually think of them as dull, faceless, boring, backwards, complex, conservative, unsuccessful, and so forth.

With so many organizations calling for people's time, energy, and resources, the brands that communicate their personality effectively are often the ones that best resonate with supporters.

Capturing and Communicating a Captivating Personality

The first step in capturing and developing a captivating Brand Personality is to take an audience-centered approach. That is, do your homework (which ideally includes research) to gain intimate knowledge of your supporters' and your potential supporters' behaviors, needs, and goals.

Uniqueness and authenticity are central to developing affirmation and passion for your cause and purpose. A Brand Personality can't simply be layered on. It should permeate the organization, affecting operational policies, hiring, staff attitudes, and even organizational culture. Organizational behavior is the foundation from which an organization can build the outward expression of its Brand Personality.

Be Consistent and Be Loved

Building a strong and effective Brand Personality usually means aligning all brand touchpoints with which your priority constituents interact. Whether it's how visitors are treated when they visit your facility or the look, feel, and distribution method of your annual report, you have many opportunities to build, strengthen, and reinforce your Brand Personality through consistent communications.

Managing consistency usually means being consistent in the way your brand looks (visuals), the way it sounds (tone), and the way it interacts (staff and volunteer encounters).

The National Geographic Society, an exploration and environmental nonprofit founded in 1888, is a remarkable brand when it comes to consistency and success. Their "yellow" rectangle had its roots in their monthly magazine but is now applied elegantly and wisely to everything from a cable TV network to bags at their gift shop. They are not only one of the most recognized brands, but supporters sign up for offerings, events, and activities as diverse as media and entertainment, exploration vacations, and photography equipment. They are so good at communicating and branding that many people don't often realize they're supporting a cause when they buy one of their products or buy into one of their offerings. People enjoy supporting National Geographic's mission so much, it doesn't even feel as if they're sacrificing to do so. Can you imagine the success you'd have if your supporters felt that way?

What Does Your Brand Say When It's Not Even Talking?

Visual information is the quickest and most noticeable way to convey Brand Personality. Tangible touchpoints such as your website, brochures, videos, and building signage are some of the more obvious places where Brand Personality can be conveyed through color, contrast, and even typeface. But your reception and lobby areas, staff name badges, and uniforms or wardrobe are also important parts of the mix. More than simple aesthetics, these visual expressions can be highly symbolic of your brand's personality and authenticity.

Two good brands to compare are Patagonia and The North Face. Not only are they both consumer brands known to do good, they are highly competitive brands selling very similar goods. If you visit their webpages, you'll note Patagonia wears "doing good" on their sleeves and it's working. In a recent poll of favorable brand reputations, Patagonia is at the top of the list. Their site is colorful and focuses on kids, friends, and the places and causes that are important to them.

Contrast Patagonia's website with that of The North Face. The North Face is all business with detailed gear imagery and high-adrenaline photography of people in challenging, mountaintop environments. Instead of encouraging people to "feel good by doing good" as Patagonia advocates, The North Face wants its brand loyalists to "never stop exploring."

Both have equal validity and are likely very profitable, but the position they each take, though both do good, has put Patagonia at the top of the brand reputation charts while The North Face isn't even on the top 100 list.

Every aspect of your messaging matters as they all send cues and information to your audience about who you are as an organization, what is important to you, and what you stand for.

Ask yourself what the visual cues are that you are sending out and if they match your desired Brand Personality.

Are You in Tune with Your Tone?

Whether it's written or verbal, an organization's tone of voice is communicated with each internal and external interaction. Whatever you determine your organization's tone of voice needs to be, it's important that your organization sound human and be consistent.

As far as the tone you should adopt, think about your overall Brand Personality and choose one that fits. Some options include casual, friendly, clever, cool, professional, helpful, smart, and honest. Sometimes using a "this but not that" list helps further define your tone. For example, your tone can be "informal but not careless" or "expert but not bossy."

Obviously there are times when you need to adjust your tone of voice. Flexibility is not only important so that your Brand Personality doesn't come across as robotic or automated. It's also needed so you can adapt to different circumstances and to the emotional state of your audience.

The Heritage Foundation is a public policy think tank in Washington, D.C., that essentially defines the conservative voice in American politics. The ACLU (American Civil Liberties Union) arguably is the leading voice for progressives in American political and legal policy- and lawmaking. Both of these organizations make essentially the same "our rights are under attack" argument daily to their priority constituents and supporters.

Though they're both "fighting for your rights," they both know how to express their brands in words and images that send signals to their respective targets. The Heritage Foundation uses words such as freedom and prosperity and describes the opposition as radical and extreme, while the ACLU talks to their audiences about rights and advocacy and labels their enemies as threatening and inhumane.

Both of these brands clearly take on an appropriately serious tone. They both are, in an ideals sense, seemingly fighting for the same things. But their targets, messages, and approaches could not be more different. However, they both agree on one thing: Their cause is serious, and it requires a combative, serious tone to advance their agendas and garner the support needed to do so.

Your Brand Is Filled with Personalities

An organization's leadership, staff, and volunteers play a big role in communicating your Brand Personality. To begin, it's good to recruit people who you believe fit the personality of your brand. Beyond that, training is important to maintain consistency; however, be careful not to rely on scripted interactions and overly restrictive guidelines.

The best way to communicate an authentic Brand Personality is to educate your staff about your brand values and voice and then allow them to deliver your message in their own unique ways.

Key Steps to Building a Brand Personality

1. Formulate your brand's personality by defining its values and vision.
2. Communicate your organization's personality consistently and authentically across all touchpoints.
3. Recruit staff and volunteers who align with your organization's culture and character.
4. Create training programs and policies that empower staff and volunteers to convey the Brand Personality in their own style.

How about your organization—does it have a clear and consistent Brand Personality? If so, own it, teach it, and share it ... and then you'll be in a better position to do more good.

CHAPTER 27

Brand Naming: What's in a (Brand) Name?

A Great Name Is Like Having Extra Horsepower

Having a complicated, boring, generic, or soundalike name generally won't stop a brand from achieving success, but it can definitely impede its growth and be a drag on its potential.

Obviously, if you're starting a new organization or providing a new service, naming should be one of the first branding components you consider, and it's a great (and inexpensive) way to create differentiation.

If your product, service, or brand has a name that you believe is undifferentiated or not memorable, you may want to consider modifying it or changing it. While your current name may have some equity with certain audiences, it may be costing you more than what you could gain with a new name. The Lance Armstrong Foundation, an organization that raises money for cancer research, successfully changed its name to Livestrong Foundation after its namesake was found to have used performance-enhancing drugs throughout his career. The World Wrestling Federation (WWF) changed its name to

World Wrestling Entertainment (WWE) after being sued by another WWF, the World Wildlife Fund, a nonprofit global conservation organization founded in 1961, which sued them for trademark infringement. And Ally Financial made a very successful transition away from GMAC Finance because of limitations and associations with GM (General Motors).

Great names have certain qualities. They are:

- **Memorable**–They stick in your brain and stand out in the marketplace.
- **Meaningful**–They align with what you do or provide—or with the personality of your organization.
- **Readable**–They are easy to spell and certainly easy to pronounce.
- **Distinctive**–They are unique and create separation from other like organizations.

Name. Brand.

If you have a big marketing and branding budget, you can overcome a bad or dull name with compelling messages. But most nonprofits don't have that luxury. As such, having an unforgettable and unique name is a strategic advantage and increases the efficiency of your messaging.

Here are some things to consider when developing a distinctive brand name:

- **Literal or descriptive names** are easily copied and imitated, which can lead to market and audience confusion.
- **Obscure and emotional names** create separation and natural interest in your brand (think about Google, Yahoo!, and Apple).
- **Generic and copycat names** cost more to build, aren't compelling, and will likely drown in the sea of sameness.

Generating a Name That Lasts for Generations

I've personally been involved in naming projects for over thirty years. The approach I've developed for naming has been successfully employed for everything from Fortune 500 companies to small, local companies (and everything in between). The following eight-step process outlines what I consider to be the best practices for generating a strong and lasting name.

The first three steps of this process outline the criteria for the ideal name; the rest provide process steps for choosing the best name:

1. Define the essence (meaning, key benefit, spirit, heart, and soul) of your organization, product, or service.
2. List the qualities (traits, personality, distinctiveness) that the name must represent.
3. Identify the perceptions and expectations the name should create for contacts.
4. Create a range of possible directions guided by the preceding considerations.
   Step four can be done as a group or as individuals who then reconvene with the group to share ideas. The efforts of step four should generate from fifty to one hundred possible names.
5. Screen each potential name through the following:
6. The first phase of this screening process will require a group to discuss the *denotative* (literal meaning) and *connotative* (suggested meaning) of each potential name. Hone down the list to no more than twenty-five names for which you will conduct legal and linguistic checks. These are the steps in the initial screening process:
   - Denotative meaning
   - Connotative meaning
   - Legal check

- Linguistic check (for brands with an international presence)
7. Use a "Naming Scoresheet" like the following one to evaluate the names that make it through this screening process (usually ten to fifteen). Then run the remaining names through a scoring process based on these "great name qualities":
    - Memorability
    - Readability
    - Meaningfulness
    - Uniqueness

This is usually done by having each member of the group score each individual name on a scale from one to five (with one being the lowest), then calculating the highest scoring names to arrive at your "Top 5" or "Top 10" names.

Again, keep people objective by not allowing them to calculate the totals for each name on the scoresheet. Otherwise, people tend to jockey their scoring to make sure the names they like finish higher than ones they don't prefer.

As I've mentioned previously, these kinds of decisions cannot come down to like/don't like voting outcomes. A name has a job to do, so voting on names as you would job candidates needing to have certain qualifications is better than turning the process into a popularity contest. It would be unprofessional to do so.

NAMING SCORESHEET

Please rate each name in each category. A rating of "1" is low, "5" is very high.

	Name	Meaningful	Memorable	Readable	Unique	Total Score
1						
2						
3						
4						
5						
6						
7						
8						
9						

8. The final step includes talking with sample members of your target audience—conducting primary research on each existing/potential name to test with these questions:
    - Is the name in sync with the overall objectives and goals of the organization?
    - Does the name command attention?
    - Is the name in sync with the organization's image and key messages?
    - Does the name have any negative or positive connotations?

While your name is important, your brand
cannot survive on your name alone.
How your brand is executed *and* the strength of your name are
both vital components for a successful and sustained branding
effort. A great brand name can serve as an anchor for your mission,
a symbol of your story, a point of difference, a memory trigger, or
just an element that provides an "extra kick" for your branding and
marketing program.

CHAPTER 28

Brand Visual Identity: What Signals Are You Sending?

The Six Elements of an Effective Visual Identity

An effective visual identity is one that sends visual signals that reinforce the perceptions that your brand wants to own. For example, if your brand wants to own a perception of trust, blue reinforces that signal; red sends different signals—energy, danger, strength, power, determination, and passion. By being intentional about the use of these visual elements, your communications will reinforce your brand.

Symbol: You Need to Make Your Mark

A great logo is first—it's the indispensable articulation of your brand identity. It's the Cornerstone for the rest of the building, but it's not the only visual symbol that identifies your organization.

Typography: It's Not Just What You Say, But How You Say It

The typeface you use says as much about your organization as the words you use—and sometimes more. Designers today can choose from hundreds of thousands of typefaces that range from crisp and proper faces such as Didot to grungy and distressed, such as Urban Jungle.

The fonts you use need to accurately communicate the personality of your brand and signal its degree of formality, approachability, and/or history.

Typefaces are like actors with human voices: they can be gruff, gravelly, or uncouth. They can be graceful, musical, or light. So be sure that the typefaces you choose convey the proper tone.

Finally, be mindful of the application. Stick with a font family that works well for display: short, visually impactful uses such as video titles or brochure headlines. Choose a different, more legible and restrained family of fonts to represent you for longer communication, such as brochure body copy or content on your website.

Information System: Where Everything Falls into Place

In simple terms, an information system is a clearly defined structure for the visual elements of your communication. The information system provides the logic for where elements appear, how big they are, and how much space they have around them. The information system is the framework that provides consistency across innumerable documents created by innumerable people. This consistent, repeatable look-and-feel creates recognition within your messaging, increasing the frequency of impressions. And as you've already seen me state many times—frequency wins!

Color: When It Comes to Your Brand, Hue Is Huge

Quick, what is McDonald's color? What color is Lowe's? What color is Target's? And T-Mobile's? Chances are good you said something like, "yellow, blue, red, and hot pink." That's because these brands have defined a key color to represent their brand, and they always use it.

Start with the color (or colors) found in your logo and use it consistently and accurately. For example, my company's logo uses PMS 640 and PMS 8401 for the gray portions. Our communications, from postcards and business cards to presentation materials, always include these same colors.

Be careful though . . . if you set all forty pages of your annual report in the sunshine yellow from your logo, it will not only be illegible, it will likely give readers a massive headache! So it's helpful to define a few acceptable and complementary colors that can be used (sparingly) in conjunction with your primary brand colors.

Finally, when it comes to color, you need to be exact: no guessing, no eyeballing. Use specific color formulations based on your execution: PMS or CMYK for print and RGBA or hexadecimal for onscreen use. Because there's no "close enough" when it comes to your brand.

Imagery: Imagine People Not Reading Any of Your Copy

This is where many, *many* organizations stumble. The images you use on your website and in your collateral reinforce perceptions of your brand—but they can more easily undermine it. So just as you carefully define acceptable fonts and colors, you need to define acceptable imagery. That includes appropriate subject matter as well as the photographic or illustrative style.

Even more importantly, the images you choose should define *your* organization—not *any* organization. How many times have you used a stock photo and then saw the same photo in another brochure or on another site? While original photography is an expense, it also results in imagery that perfectly expresses your brand and belongs only to you.

Access: Brand Knowledge Is Brand Power

We've unpacked *five* of the elements of visual identity, but there's another crucial component of a visual identity: understanding.

Most improper executions of visual identity result from ignorance, not malevolence. Or more bluntly: It's easy to go wrong if you don't know what's right. So after you've defined the fonts, colors, imagery, and geometric structure that make up your visual identity, share that information. Thorough brand standards are a good thing—but not if they're sitting on a shelf in a three-ring binder that no one ever opens!

Take the time to explain to your team—and not just your marketing department—what your standards are. Trust me: Thirty minutes spent explaining your visual identity system can eliminate days of misspent labor and thousands of misspent dollars.

When you've explained the system, make those standards easily available. Save a PDF on a shared drive or on your intranet. Build a web page and have everyone bookmark the link. Do what's easy, because if you make your visual identity system simple to use, people will more easily execute your standards.

CHAPTER 29

Brand Logo: Make Your Mark

A Good Logo Makes Doing Good Easier

A logo is like a face; it's a visual identifier that helps others remember who you are. And the easier it is to remember your organization's identity and name, the simpler it is for people to help you do good work...and tell others about you and what you're doing.

Logos come in many shapes, sizes, and colors. They typically are formed using a mark, flag, symbol, or signature. Rarely does a logo visually describe what the organization does—its job is to identify your organization, not explain it.

What Makes a Logo Good?

Most experts agree that a good logo is distinctive, appropriate, graphically simple, easy to work with, and easy to read.

To ensure you have a strong logo, put it through the following five filters:

1. **Is it simple?** Less complicated and clean logos help an organization stand out.
2. **Is it memorable?** Good logos are instantly recognizable, even when you drive by them at seventy miles per hour.

3. **Is it practical?** Your logo must work in a variety of sizes, mediums, and applications.
4. **Is it meaningful?** A good logo is one that fits with the organization's Brand Personality and, ideally, it helps convey what sets the organization apart. Remember, your aim is to convey a distinguishing factor, not the product you sell or the service you provide.
5. **Is it timeless?** Trendy logos tend to get dated quickly. Keep yours simple and save yourself the need to update it too soon and too often.

Good Logos Are Agile

A logo may be a source of pride and beauty, but it also needs to be practical and functional. So before you select a logo, ask yourself if it is still effective when:

- It is printed in one color.
- It is printed very small.
- It is printed very big.
- It is printed in reverse (light on a dark background).
- It is printed in vertical or horizontal formats.

Do Your Best and Learn from the Best

Fortunately, it isn't very hard to do solid research on good logos. We're all exposed to many (actually, thousands of) logos every day. And while there may be differences of opinion as to what a good logo is and what it is not, we can all learn from the top national brands with highly recognizable logos.

Some successful logo changes include McDonald's simplification to using the "golden arches" for its identity, Federal Express moving to FedEx for its name and logo, and the updates made over the years to Starbucks and Apple logos, which are models for how best to update an identity to stay relevant without losing brand equity. Apple, as you may recall, had a multicolored striped logo and it's simplified that to using just one color (usually either white or black depending on the background). Not only was this easier to reproduce, but this fits more with Apple's clean, cool, and contemporary brand. Starbucks also cleaned up its logo over time and removed the somewhat controversial spread-finned legs of its mermaid icon, focusing more on her face.

A few logo fails included GAP Inc. moving from its iconic blue box logo to a generic, black and white typeface for its identity (and then reverting back). This change demonstrated a misunderstanding of what it takes to be a leading fashion brand. JC Penney's attempt to become known as JCP through a logo change made it difficult to understand and connect to a well-established name brand.

After years of observation and work on helping to create logos, I've discovered that many of the world's most recognizable logos have several things in common. Here are what they include:

- Their shape—and sometimes even their name—does *not* indicate what they make, sell, do, or offer.
- Symbols are *not* used by many top brands, just a typeface with the words of the company name, and the fonts used tend to be clean and simple.
- One word (at the most two) or an acronym is used in most of the world's top brand logos.
- Bylines or taglines are rarely included or featured with the logo.
- Key colors are red, blue, yellow, and orange. In each category, competitive leaders each own one, or a unique combination, of these colors.

Note: Green has come on strong recently as another key color used among brand leaders (probably because of its eco-friendly cues). But use caution when choosing any color for your brand, especially based on trendiness. Today's green may become yesterday's periwinkle!

CHAPTER 30

Brand Voice: Be More Painkiller, Less Vitamin

It's more important than ever for nonprofit leaders to be good stewards of dollars and resources used for growing awareness and support. In our current pandemic-shaped and media-saturated world, it's essential. One of the keys to being a good steward is to spend less time and money on messaging that doesn't resonate with your donor audiences.

The news cycle has become seemingly endless doom and gloom. Fear and negativity dominate discussions of all kinds, and there seems to be no end in sight to our high-tension atmosphere and divisiveness. During these times, people want solutions, and they want to know there are difference-makers out there.

The author of the international bestselling book *Sell Like Crazy*, Sabri Suby, who heads Australia's fastest-growing digital marketing agency, wrote in a social media post how brands can be a ray of sunshine in the storm and can thrive during times like these.[27]

He said the secret is to understand that in tough moments, people don't want candy or vitamins. Rather, they are looking for a painkiller.

Candylike brands and candy messaging are representative of organizations that are very nice and that people enjoy, but they aren't positioning themselves as a solution to a burning problem. So while they can get support during good times, they're not seen as essential in more challenging seasons.

Examples of nonprofit "candy" brands are fine arts organizations, theater groups, symphonies, galleries, performing arts venues, zoos, and planting trees. While many people feel strongly about the need for these enriching activities and events (count me in that crowd), they're not universally seen as essential to support when times get tough.

Vitaminlike organizations are known to have a very positive impact over time, but they're also not seen as solving issues of urgent need. Therefore, like candy organizations, they are not positioned well to grow during economic contractions.

Examples of nonprofit "vitamin" brands are hiking trail associations, after-school activities, junior athletic programs, nature preserves, museums, and fitness programs. These would all fit into the vitamin cause category. They're all seen as good for participating individuals, but they're not perceived as critical.

Painkiller brands and messaging, in contrast, are seen as coming from causes that offer immediate solutions to vitally important and pressing problems. These are problems that the majority of donors recognize and agree need to be alleviated promptly and urgently.

Examples of nonprofit painkiller organizations are those dealing with hunger, emergency housing, healthcare, and community safety. These are all painkiller causes that thrive during tough times. Painkiller organizations are seen as solving urgent issues. They are perceived as critically important—now.

Tough Times Require Tougher Stances

Suby also says when situations are dire, you don't want to position your organization as anything *but* a painkiller. Think about it this way, he says: "If you're feeling crippling pain, your focus goes quickly to finding immediate solutions."[28]

In other words, you might be a vitamin type of cause, but you'd better find someone or something you serve that has an urgent need or you will miss "moments of opportunity" during challenging times to capture attention and support when people likely have more time and empathy than they do during stronger economic cycles.

At the beginning of the COVID-19 pandemic, Lisa Sherman from The Ad Council noted: "This is a moment of irreversible empathy. As the number of people who find themselves in tough situations soars . . . so does the number of people who understand at a visceral level what instability feels like."[29]

Painkillers Are Always Needed

Charity Water is an organization often admired for its messaging and positioning. One of the reasons it's been so successful is that its mission was founded on a painkiller platform—the recognition that many diseases being treated in Third World countries were caused by unsafe drinking water. And though it has bold goals of providing clean water for 100 million-plus people, during the height of the COVID-19 pandemic, it shifted the messaging in its ads to focus on delivering lifesaving hand sanitization resources and education for vulnerable communities. That education was about the importance of handwashing, using clean water, and killing germs, and it was a message that Americans could relate to. In short, this organization dealt with a new pain using a different painkiller message and shifted from just drinking water messaging to the need for clean water for handwashing to prevent COVID-19, as well as its ability to provide sanitation and hygiene training for people in great need.

But it's not the only organization that had timely and powerful painkiller communications resulting from a reaction to COVID-19. I've watched during the pandemic as performing arts venues encouraged people to buy gift cards to support them in a moment of great uncertainty and help support out-of-work performing artists. These venues connected the message about supporting the arts with why performing arts is an urgent need right now.

I've seen a trail association change its messaging from supporting growth to supporting maintenance and providing safe trails for people seeking a healthy escape from being in lockdown in their homes. I worked with an organization that provides deaf people with Bible translations, and I encouraged them to shift their communications focus to helping deaf people who are hungry during these difficult times—since they have language barriers, their challenges were temporarily greater to get the basic needs such as food and water.

That shift in communication focus has made these organizations' campaigns successful!

The bottom line is, when people are feeling pain, a vitamin won't provide immediate relief. Candy is out of the question. Instead, they are looking for painkillers. And while that may have been more evident during a pandemic, the reality is, there's always someone in pain and there likely is always the need to message accordingly.

What's it going to take to strengthen your messaging—another pandemic?

So how would donors characterize *your* organization?

Would they see it as candy that's sweet and nice, and an investment that tastes good and makes them feel instantly happy?

Would they see your organization as more of a vitamin that's healthy, needed in the long run, and an investment that they might make over time because they believe that it's important?

Or would your donors (and potential donors) view your organization as a painkiller that's needed *now* and communicates to them not only with urgency but as an immediate and practical solution to the problems they are already aware of?

So often it's not only a matter of who you say you are, but how you present yourself.

CHAPTER 31

Brand Tagline: Tag! You're It

Taglines: Their Roles and Importance

A tagline's job is to capture an organization's core values, brand personality, and positioning in a short, memorable, and compelling phrase. It should also be a driver of creative and themes that can speak to all the audiences you serve—both together and individually.

That's a lot to ask. And that's why creating taglines is one of the toughest tasks for any communicator and any organization.

In the consumer world, there are many very memorable taglines:

Nike | Just do it.
Apple | Think Different.
McDonald's | I'm lovin' it.
Coca-Cola | Open Happiness.
Jeep | There's Only One.

In the nonprofit world, there have been fewer memorable taglines. But some that stand out are:

United Negro College Fund | A Mind Is a Terrible Thing
to Waste.
The United Methodist Church | Open hearts. Open minds.
Open doors.
American Lung Association | Improving Life, One Breath
at a Time.
Women's Sports Foundation | Equal play.
The Salvation Army | Doing the Most Good.*

Taglines that work well are typically effective because either they
are intensely personal and motivating or they associate a brand with
higher qualities and expectations. The best taglines are affirming
and uplifting, attractive, emotive, catchy, and, of course, short, while
they also feel like a manifesto.

Six attributes to keep in mind when crafting a tagline include:

1. **It's a signature, not a headline.** Taglines usually come at the
   end of videos and at the bottom or back of print materials.
   It's easy to forget that they are a signature or crescendo or
   conclusive statement to a well-executed idea, not a headline
   or opening statement.
2. **Keep it brief.** Taglines should never be any longer than a
   sentence. Ideally, they're fewer than five words. Anything
   longer will be hard to remember.
3. **Be different.** The core purpose of a tagline is to set your
   brand apart from competitive alternatives. As such, taglines
   that suggest a difference tend to be both memorable and
   effective.

---

*   *I've been asked many times about this tagline and its similarity to my catchphrase*
DO MORE GOOD. While I can't get into details, I was contacted by an attorney
for the Salvation Army who wanted to acquire my rights to DO MORE GOOD.
When I chose not to sell or give them my rights to the trademark, they chose this
tagline workaround. It should also be noted that they are not alone in contacting
me about the DO MORE GOOD trademark; there literally have been dozens.

4. **Highlight a highlight.** If your organization has a unique feature or benefit, using a tagline to highlight its differentiation is very convincing.

5. **Evoke an emotion.** Think about your target audiences and the problems they're looking to solve. If your tagline is built from an emotional response of overcoming something or providing new or better solutions, it will likely be more emotive than other options.

6. **Commit to a commitment.** When a tagline communicates a dedication to a higher purpose, it becomes a double-edged sword—it cuts through the clutter of the marketplace and carves a strong place in the hearts of your supporters and priority constituents.

The "Don't Do It" List

According to *Nonprofit Quarterly* (NPQ), second only to your organization's name, your tagline is the most remembered, repeated message your organization will deploy. In short, a tagline is a terrible thing to waste.[30]

As challenging as it is to create a strong tagline, it's all too easy to craft one that fails. When that happens, your organization loses a potent tool and, even worse, may confuse or annoy audiences.

The NPQ says to beware of these pitfalls that can sink your tagline. So here's my "don't do it" list:

- **Don't be generic.** Be as specific and as emotive as possible to highlight a connection between an individual and your organization. Warning: Don't use generic language, which is a common error. Without embarrassing any specific organizations, here is a sample list of overly generic and uninspiring taglines:

  Hope lives here.

  Experience it.

  Bringing healing, health, and hope.

Changing lives. Building futures.

Empowering good.

A heritage of excellence.

Serving our community for over 75 years.

- **Avoid poor word choices.** They send an audience in the wrong direction. Consider this example: "Potential made possible" (an agency serving children with special needs). "Potential" and "possible" mean much the same thing. An improvement might be "Potential made accessible" or "Mission Possible."

- **Don't put two or more taglines to work (at the same time).** If you do, it will only serve to undermine your organization's brand. As a result, your audience won't get to know your organization and reinforce its brand among others. Instead, the audience will be confused, and your messaging will seem convoluted. A recent survey on nonprofit taglines had a respondent who noted this as a problem: "Various staff and board members and volunteers use different taglines."[31] In short, your choir needs to be singing from the same page, and it starts by getting them all singing from the same hymnbook.

Southwest Airlines is a brand that really understands getting everyone singing together, and sometimes their employees literally sing to their customers. Southwest's logo is a big heart, which symbolizes that the employees love what they do. Its tagline is "Low fares. Nothing to hide. That's TransFarency." It's fun, honest, atypical, and reinforces that they treat everyone the same and they're looking out for everyone's best interest. It's a high-value and high-service brand, so they know how to manage expectations and delight customers at the same time.

Test Your Taglines

Like messaging and naming, taglines should be tested with your priority constituents. In addition to standard measures such as unique, memorable, readable, and meaningful, adding catchy or sticky, motivating, and positive scoring criteria will help you evaluate and decide on the tagline that checks more boxes than others.

Again, creating a tagline isn't about being clever or funny; a tagline has a job to do and that is to help set your organization apart from alternatives in the marketplace. And most of those alternatives are likely not direct competitors. Rather, they're any company or organization competing for your audiences' discretionary time and money.

CHAPTER 32

Brand Experience: Your Brand Is What People Experience

Three Little Judgments

Everyone who comes in contact with your organization will judge it based on three factors: what they **see**, what you **say**, and what you **do**. Every engagement with your brand sends signals to the minds of the audiences. These signals shape perceptions about what your brand really stands for—and what it doesn't.

When your staff, volunteers, leadership, and even board members reinforce the same perceptions that you communicate in your messaging, then they help create positive brand associations for your publics. But if those associated with your brand don't manage those signals consistently or well in the minds of your audiences, then outside audiences will fill the gaps themselves by forming their own diverse opinions of your organization.

That's why it's so important to create a brand that not only is communicated to audiences outside the organization, but a brand that is understood by your internal audiences—so that they know how to communicate and reinforce it inside your organization as well.

Remember, a brand is made up of two simple things:

1. The promises you make.
2. The promises you keep.

That second point *sounds* simple, but it's where many brands fail because they don't meet the expectations that they have created for themselves! Nothing erodes trust and perceptions faster than not delivering on what you promise to your constituents!

In the business world, we see great examples of those who rise to the challenge of their brand promises. Jimmy Johns delivers "Freaky Fast." (One of their drivers got a speeding ticket written up in our parking lot while making a delivery to our office. I tipped the driver extra to help pay his ticket, but I also told him that the local police department might not appreciate their company's brand promise as much as I do!).

Target delivers "cheap chic," and shoppers know they will usually spend more money than they planned on when they enter their stores. One of the reasons is that Target chooses and displays products in its stores so well—with a cool, trendy style.

FedEx delivers very well on its promise that it's the one you can trust to get your package where it needs to be, "absolutely, positively overnight."

If those brands didn't keep their promises consistently, they would have failed as companies years ago.

In the nonprofit world, though, delivering on a brand promise isn't necessarily experienced first-hand. Donors only hear or read about the recipients and the benefits they receive. Since most nonprofit donors are not the direct recipients of the promises made by a nonprofit organization—and don't personally know any of the direct recipients—delivering well on "brand experience" becomes even more critical. Nonprofits need to show their donors compelling testimonials of their brand promise delivered, not just in controlled words uttered in campaigns and social media but in tangible outcomes and authentic stories that demonstrate transformation in the lives of the people and things they serve.

We're Not That Brand!

I met a "Brand Experience" expert whose whole consultancy centered on "the brand inside." He was the head of communications for a nonprofit teaching hospital with numerous specialties.

His Brand Experience story started when the hospital hired an ad agency to present new campaign ideas to them. After the agency presented its ideas, the hospital executives and communication team were all high-fiving one another, excited about this stunning new campaign.

But then, as my friend drove home that evening, he said to himself, *The hospital featured in that campaign is awesome—but we're not that hospital! Our team just said "yes" to the campaign and applauded the agency, but we can't run that campaign, because it's not us. It's just not true! Either we ditch the campaign, or we become the hospital that it describes.*

And that's exactly what they did. They ended up becoming the kind of hospital that they had wanted to advertise, which was a better hospital than they had been because they desired and were inspired to do so!

Today people fly from all over the world to be treated at this care facility.

A few years after that effort, my friend left the hospital to specialize in Brand Experience as a consultant. He became so successful that he built a custom five-million-dollar house and set it up like a boutique hotel. When you went there to work on your brand, you stayed in one of the seven suites that he used to create a memorable experience for his clients.

I started learning about his approach before I went there to work with his team for the first time. Before I arrived, I received a questionnaire asking, "What snacks do you like? What do you like to drink? What are your favorite colors? What's your favorite music? If you could choose an art style, what style would you choose?"

When I arrived, I was escorted into my room, and it was totally customized for me! In my suite, Stevie Ray Vaughn's music was playing! The kitchenette was filled with snacks I love, drinks I love, and they were well stocked! Even the comforter and pillows were reflective of my favorite colors. The art on the walls was the style I like. And there were even books on the nightstand from my favorite authors. I remember running out to the hallway saying, "You can't believe what's going on in my room!" The other people staying there as part of our group all met me there, saying, "You should come in my room! It's all about me!!"

My Brand Experience friend had created a memorable Brand Experience for each one of us from the first moment of arrival. When we went down to dinner that night, he asked, "How did that experience make you feel?"

We all responded by saying that it made us feel very special, "You and your team went totally out of your way to customize our rooms for each one of us." Taking the time and effort to know us before conducting business created a deeper bond immediately and allowed an openness that no amount of talking or pitching could match.

Then my Brand Experience friend added, "You wouldn't believe how unbelievably cheap it is to do that—but it made you feel like a million bucks!"

As you'd expect, he had creative standards and approaches for his practice, as well. And he had two important rules:

Rule #1: He didn't go to his clients; he made them come to him so they could experience his work and methods.

The client I was with asked during our first session, "Well, you've probably already seen some of our stores. I'd like to hear what you think."

The consultant answered, "No, I haven't been to any of your stores yet."

"You've got to be kidding me," my client said. "You haven't been to any of our stores yet? What are we paying you for?"

"No," said the consultant, "you don't understand how I work. First of all, my clients come to me. I don't go to them. And ....

"**Rule #2** is that I ask my clients to tell me what they *want* their Brand Experience to be like, and *then* I'll go to their business and tell them if what I observe and experience is anything close to living up to that!"

One of the exercises that we did as a group during this time was especially insightful.

He had a hallway full of pictures of different restaurant chains, and he challenged each of us to choose one of our favorite restaurants. From there, we were instructed to pair up with another person and tell them what we love about that restaurant.

That session turned out to be the loudest, most boisterous time during our entire stay with this consultant! Then our Brand Experience expert noted, "See what happens when organizations create a great experience? You go tell other people about the experience of being there, and that testimonial is much more powerful than any ad campaign that could ever be created!"

Earlier, in the chapter about "touching every touchpoint," I provided some easy things that can be done to improve the "brand inside" your organization. It typically doesn't take a lot of effort or cost to give people a memorable experience.

Many times it's simply about making people feel special—no matter if they're donors, volunteers, staff members, or someone in need. Taking Brand Experiences to the next level also requires a strategic approach to make sure they aren't just "fun and memorable," but that they are also "on brand." That means they reinforce something meaningful about your brand story.

Anyone who comes in contact with your organization shouldn't just hear why you're different—they should authentically *feel* that difference too. And then they can authentically tell their friends about it with genuine enthusiasm!

Brand Experience can help turn your organization's friends into raving fans—donors, volunteers, contributors, beneficiaries, and anyone else who can recommend your nonprofit to others and tell them how wonderful you are based on positive experiences they've had personally.

Remember, your donors and friends have choices: they can choose involvement in your nonprofit because you ring all their bells, *or* they can donate and volunteer with another organization that delivers better on their brand promise.

And don't forget that your beneficiaries may someday turn into volunteers or donors. They should be treated as well as you treat donors—show them sincere appreciation for their abilities. Consider how transparency helps you with your mission and vision, as does gratitude for everyone. And you need communication that gives voice to that gratitude.

Keep in mind that your brand experiences don't begin with outsiders; they begin with internal staff. Make sure your team is a cohesive unit to drive strong brand-enhancing and reinforcing behavior and actions. Communicating expectations as Brand Experience enhancements can also promote a richer culture where employees and volunteers can consistently carry out your brand's objectives and understand they're contributing to something bigger than just themselves.

Give Me an "E!"

The "5E Model" is an acronym often used in consumer branding to design meaningful services, events, and learning experiences for your constituents. This model can help you communicate the Brand Experience concept and its importance to growing your mission. The 5E Model is also useful to help you align a team, access collective creativity, and create leadership models that enable collaboration. It is an integrative model that can add coherence, elegance, and excitement to the experience of engagement with your nonprofit. It is also a framework for building holistic and meaningful donor experiences.

The 5E Model was first invented in 1994 by Larry Keeley, a strategist and innovation guru, and cofounder of Doblin Inc, which is now Deloitte Consulting.[32] And organizations like Kaopilot[33] have since evolved this model:

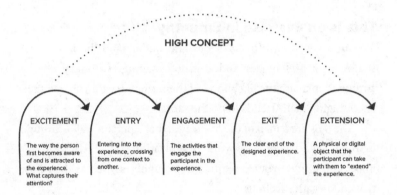

The overarching umbrella in this model is the "High Concept"— which is the premise of the kind of Brand Experience you want to create and the "Meaningful Outcomes" you want to achieve.

Originally, the film industry invented the idea of a High Concept to organize the creativity of many people into the creation of a coherent story, like a red thread that runs through and ties together all the pieces.[34]

Once you know your Brand Experience High Concept (which is likely and ideally something that is inspired by your Brand Promise), you can now start designing the Brand Experience "Journey" for your participants. Each of these steps is important in designing a Brand Experience for your constituents:

1. Excitement
2. Entry

3. Engagement
4. Exit
5. Extension

To really delight and retain donors and volunteers, we need to become experts on the journey that each person walks—from having never heard of your organization to becoming "evangelists" for it.

This Is an Exercise in Empathy

Step into your constituents' shoes and understand the forces that shape their preferences and decision-making. Ultimately, we're aiming to increase the likelihood of them staying with you and then encouraging their friends to do the same.

The 5 Es are a map of the five stages that a person walks through in their experiences with your organization. For each stage, it's important to note your constituents' thoughts, as well as their positive and negative feelings.

First, map out the "as-is" process, creating a picture of what that journey looks like for your constituents today. Once you have an accurate understanding, then you can play around with "what-if" ways to improve it.

Let's look at each E in more detail. Ask yourself these questions:

Excitement—How will people first hear about us?
- What entices them to learn more? What triggers their interest?

Entry—What impression do we create for new people when they walk into our office or find our website?
- Think about all the senses: what do they hear, smell, and feel? How are the lights and the chair they sit on?
- What are the colors of our website and the layout? How intuitive is the navigation?

Engagement—How does this interaction usually play out?
- Are we laying the foundations for a long, personal relationship?
- Will they come back to our website or events more than once before they decide to become donors?
- Do they need to talk with a person, or is the process entirely automated?

Exit—What impression is our constituent left with?
- After checking out our website or attending one of our events, do they leave with a bad taste in their mouth, or are they excited and empowered?
- Are they treated well with prompt and friendly follow-up after they make a donation, or are they forgotten?

Extension—What triggers a repeat engagement?
- Do our constituents tell their friends about us?
- What sort of interaction will they have with us in the future?[35]

Make People Feel the Good— Don't Just Talk about It

I witnessed a great example of Brand Experience personally one Christmas Eve morning when I received a call from Rev. Layman at Mel Trotter Rescue Mission. He was a client whose ministry we'd helped grow, and he asked, "Are you in the office today? And your staff, are they there too? Because I'd like to invite you to all come down the street and take a tour of our new Women's and Children's Center."

Since it was Christmas Eve, I decided it would be a nice break for our entire staff to get out of the office and tour the new facility that we helped to raise money for.

Rev. Layman met us in the lobby and, right away, you could see he was delighted. It was his dream to better serve homeless women and children in our community. Not only was it a growing need but building a new facility like this was something this rescue mission had never done before in its ninety-five-year history.

Rev. Layman was proud to show us not just the facility, but how it was constructed with the "customer experience" in mind. He equated the lobby to a place that welcomed families as if they were going to a nice hotel. Each room was created to keep the family together and offered heightened levels of privacy not typically offered to residents of a rescue mission. He noted that it was his goal to give families *more* than just a place to stay. He wanted them to feel welcomed, and not homeless.

Beyond creating a Brand Experience for the beneficiaries, he used these tours to create a memorable experience for those who had helped make this facility possible. While our firm and staff were really just "hired hands" who'd helped raise awareness and the needed funds, Rev. Layman knew we did our work with a deep commitment to doing anything and everything needed to help reach their goals.

As he walked us through the beautiful, five-story facility, every time we ran into a staff person or beneficiary, he would introduce my team with, "These good people made this new center possible."

He intentionally chose not to introduce us as paid consultants; instead, he elevated our contributions as one of a special group of people who made this dream come true and had partnered with him to make this incredibly important facility possible.

Again and again, to person after person, Rev. Layman repeated, "These good people made this new center possible!"

By the time we finished the tour, everyone on my team was wiping away tears! Their hearts were touched by Rev. Layman's words and his appreciation for the role we had played. And to see the center in action, with homeless women and children finding shelter in this beautiful new facility—it was an emotional experience for all of us and one of the best Christmas gifts we ever received as a company! It wasn't just that we helped raise money to build the center, but every person on our creative team realized then that they had played an active role in helping to transform people's lives.

Rev. Layman, whether he realized it or not, used the 5E Model that day:

1. **Excitement:** He called us on Christmas Eve and invited us to leave the office and pay him a holiday visit!

2. **Entry:** He personally welcomed us into the new Women's and Children's Center, and from the lobby forward, he showed us around with pride!

3. **Engagement:** He drew us in, not only to see the center in action, but to hear how much our contribution was appreciated and valued!

4. **Exit:** We were touched and moved by the experience, and we were left with incredibly warm feelings that have stayed with us for years!

5. **Extension:** My team members and I were much more likely to spread the news about Mel Trotter Rescue Mission and share with our family members and friends over the holidays what we had seen, done, and experienced!

That's what great Brand Experiences do for a nonprofit organization. They not only feel good, but they also cause others to do and want to do *more* good.

PART V

ACTION

IDEAS PROCESS
A = Action

I was working with a client who led a nonprofit marriage counseling program for couples who were close to filing for a divorce. It was an intensive, two weekend program with a triage approach where multiple counselors came together to help couples work through the myriad issues that were driving them to a point of desperation.

As we explored possible messaging opportunities, we found their 80 percent marriage-saving rate to be very compelling. So we centered much of the campaign around that success rate and how it could give hope to seemingly lost causes.

The ads and communication materials we created were initially very effective at driving interest, clicks, and website visits. However, the closing rate (couples signing up and paying for the program) was lower than anticipated.

When sitting in a meeting with the client, strategizing ways we could improve the campaign's closing rate performance, one of client's staff members said, "Yeah, the program is expensive—four thousand—but husbands would easily spend that on a big screen TV, and they won't invest it to save their marriage." That prompted me to think about all my years of marketing big-ticket retail merchandise. I learned the best way to turn interest into revenue is to lower the perceived cost of acquisition. In other words, make the offer seem more affordable.

I threw out the solution of offering no-interest financing, low payment options, and even partial cash back refunds when couples completed the program. These offers worked, and significantly increased the number of sign-ups and conversions.

Getting people to take action often requires creative thinking and solutions. Sometimes blending for-profit concepts into a nonprofit program or borrowing closing ideas from other industries and applying them to your situation can be a difference-maker.

And when the differences made are things like saved marriages and happier families, why not work to find new ways to take action and do more good.

CHAPTER 33

Marketing Investment: Why Don't Nonprofits Invest in Their Brands?

With all the important organizational growth-enhancing information we've reviewed thus far, it seems obvious that branding and marketing your brand should be seen as wise investments. However, many nonprofits and their boards continue to view these as either unnecessary expenses or necessary evils that are a frustrating money pit.

One of the reasons nonprofits shy away from investing in marketing is that, for years, many charity-rating services and charity watchdogs have lowered a nonprofit organization's evaluation scores if, in its opinion, the nonprofit invested too heavily in marketing. They believed that such expenses didn't advance or help the cause of the organization.

Fortunately, that has been changing.
According to an article in *The New York Times,* Charity Navigator, the largest site evaluating nonprofits, has been overhauling its rating system. Its goal, according to the article, is to "wean donors off a reliance on administrative-cost ratios and other financial metrics."[36]

Critics of nonprofit rating services such as Charity Navigator have long maintained that choosing a charity based on low administrative costs is a poor way for potential donors to judge where their donations would do the most good. A philanthropy consultant cited in this same article said that this standard was "detrimental to the nonprofit sector" and that "it encourages donors to steer resources toward organizations pushing everything into the cause, rather than investing in ... things that make a nonprofit strong."[37]

Adding fuel to the fire.

Now that we've established that marketing an organization's brand is an important investment on many levels, let me turn up the heat and clarify why it's not just important, but a *necessary* investment.

First, let me introduce you to one of my favorite statements about branding. It happens to be intellectual property of my firm and has resided in many presentations we've given: *"Your brand will happen **by you**, or it will happen **to you**."*

Basically we've been advising our clients that you have a brand— whether you invest in it or not. As such, you can either choose to manage and proactively market your brand—or not. Either way, your brand *happens*.

Once in a meeting with a client, we were sitting in our conference room and had just recommended that our client start a social media page on an emerging platform.

The client questioned the need for adding this to their social media mix and gave us quite a strong pushback argument. Their rationale was that their audience was too mature for this particular platform, and it would stretch their limited internal resources to develop and manage content for this medium. They added anecdotal evidence that their key audiences didn't even really use social media. All solid considerations, but while sitting in the meeting with them, one of my younger staff members went to the social media platform in discussion, searched the client's brand, and pulled up an existing page, using their logo, that had already been created and launched by someone who was not part of their organization. So their brand was already happening and living on this platform, but the client's brand managers were not controlling it!

Fortunately for them, it was a "fan" of the organization who had taken it upon themselves to launch and maintain "branded" content on this new platform. But the client didn't even know this page existed!

Imagine if that were not the case—if a detractor launched a "brand" page on an emerging platform, and they were communicating negative information about the cause and its work?

Today that client actively controls its own content and manages its brand quite diligently on all social platforms using software that make it easy to do so. They learned, happily not the hard way, that their brand does indeed happen, and that an organization must do everything it can to make sure it is managing and controlling every vehicle for advancing the cause and mission of the organization.

Fanning the Flames

In Seth Godin's book *The Purple Cow*, he says the number of choices people have keeps increasing, while the amount of time they have to consider their choices keeps decreasing. He ultimately concludes that brands that fail to be "remarkable" (like the sight of a purple cow in a meadow would be) will struggle to thrive and grow.[38]

Add to that the nonprofit sector's explosive growth rate of 20 percent over the last ten years, in contrast to a growth rate of about 2–3 percent in the for-profit sector.[39] Note: That's a growth rate of nearly *ten times* more than the for-profit market.

Which means, while people already have an incredible number of choices competing for their discretionary time and money from the consumer market, now they have ever-expanding choices—20 percent more just in the last decade—for places they can donate and volunteer.

Making the competitive voices environment even more difficult, it is estimated that by 2030, the average person will own fifteen connected devices.[40] This will lead not only to even more diversions and distractions, but it will make it harder for people to unplug and disconnect from work and other obligations. Plus, marketers of consumer products are busy forging plans and technology to tap into all these devices to grow and convey their messages. In short, competition for time and attention will only get more challenging in the years ahead.

Is It Getting Hot in Here?

Hopefully you recall my friend Ken Calwell who heads marketing and innovation for Compassion International and had a highly decorated career serving several major consumer brands. One day on a phone call, comparing notes in preparation for him to speak at a DO MORE GOOD conference, I brought up Godin's *Purple Cow* point and added Peter Drucker's "The single purpose of a non-profit is to create a supporter" statement.

Talking about these concepts prompted Ken to say something that I consider extremely profound: "My observation is that it is critical for a nonprofit to see themselves as a catalyst, a connector . . . not the cause." They are the tool that can be used to make a difference in a particular issue, but they are not the issue itself.

CHAPTER 34

Media Strategies: You Are a Media Channel

Once upon a time, nonprofits could live and even thrive on a well-placed story in the media or from a PSA (public service announcement) that ran in prime time or on the evening news. For those of you who don't know what that means, you're likely in a generation where digital media has been prevalent most of your pre-adult and adult life. But for many people, there was a time when "traditional" media (broadcast television and radio, as well as daily printed newspapers) dominated the communication landscape.

What's happened since then is that even traditional media have entered the digital world, and we're living in a time when anyone can be a media content creator. It also means no one is sitting around and waiting to get the news when it comes on at 6 p.m. Instead, it is fed to us all day and night via "breaking news alerts" on multiple devices.

The proliferation of information not only has created a media- and information-saturated world, it has created a lot of freedom and potential. No longer is there a bottleneck of journalists and editors blocking the gateway to getting news and information to our priority constituents. And because digital platforms today collect so much information on their users, targeting your messaging has never been more precise.

The reality is, while it's easy to complain about how hard it is to cut through the clutter and noise created by all these digital and social platforms, it's never been easier or more efficient to reach your potential and engaged audiences.

The Press Release Is Dead

It's not that traditional media outlets don't still have power and impact; many still do. However, getting "coverage" today is more and more a "pay to play" situation. That means if you're not an advertiser or willing to pay for a feature segment (which are essentially advertorials), then your chances of getting time and/or attention from traditional media today are slim to none.

And let's say you do score a coveted "free segment," the cost and effort to securing such coverage usually far outweigh what you can do on your own, through your own media channels.

The New Big Three

The old media "Big Three" used to be the broadcast television networks of ABC, NBC, and CBS. What they released was consumed by the masses and bought, sold, and talked about the next day. The new "Big Three" today are arguably Facebook, Instagram, and YouTube (and by the time we turn around, it may have changed again to TikTok, Snapchat, and WhatsApp).

While leading media outlets continue to evolve and change, the Big Three, when it comes to reaching and engaging your audience, will always need to be "quantity, quality, and variety," regardless of which platforms you use to communicate.

Many social media and digital content experts talk about things such as user video and viral and shareable content, but those are really *tactics* looking for a strategy. Instead, make it your goal to be aggressive in your online content efforts and to increase the quantity, quality, and variety of your digital and social media posts. If you judiciously create posts that are worth the read or view (informative vs. informational), that is, giving your audience something they can use, rather than just facts that are irrelevant to their lives, then you will be a difference-maker for your organization.

All this is to say, it is no longer a safe or smart bet to work to gain coverage through traditional media channels. Instead you should be investing your organization's time, talent, and resources to connect with and grow your audiences on platforms that you control and manage.

Different Media. Different Audiences. Different Messages.

There are plenty of tools that can help you manage and coordinate all your different social media platforms easily and efficiently. But there is always the temptation to handle them all the same way—and that would be a huge mistake. An even bigger mistake would be believing that your organization needs to be participating on *every* platform. The reality is, different platforms speak to different audiences in different ways, and you need to determine which ones are right for your audiences and your organization.

Some (admittedly, overly) simple guidelines are:

- Facebook is the biggest (for now), but it's mainly for people over forty. It's also more text-based and less visual than other platforms.
- Instagram is the second biggest (for now). It is far more visual than Facebook and appeals mainly to people over eighteen but under forty-five.
- YouTube is for everyone and is all about video content. Chances are, the younger you are, the more you rely on

YouTube for almost all your news, entertainment, and web information needs.

- Snapchat and TikTok are for teens, pre-teens, college students, and adults in their twenties (as well as parents and creepers checking out those audiences). Snapchat is for insider communication within private friend groups, and TikTok is a platform for making and sharing short-form videos, in genres such as dance, comedy, and education.

- Twitter is for those interested in following celebrities, news personalities, professional athletes, and politicians. It is almost exclusively text based and appeals to audiences who like to share theological and intellectual ideas, as well as links to sometimes controversial articles, videos, and ideas.

- Pinterest is mainly for women who love fashion, food, and decorating, but it has been growing among men who like cars and outdoor activities. Like Instagram, Pinterest is very visual and is becoming a fast-growing marketplace for products and trends. Unlike other platforms, it is very "hobby or special interest" oriented.

- LinkedIn is for professionals and, quietly, has become a great place to reach upscale executives and those on their way up the corporate ladder.

Give It a Boost

Shockingly, just because you've built a following on a few platforms doesn't mean you're consistently able to reach those audiences with your posts! As a matter of fact, recent estimates are that you're reaching fewer than 10 percent of your followers with any average post. Why? Because that's one way these platforms make money—they charge you to reach the audiences that you helped them to cultivate! You can get angry about it . . . or you can just give your posts an occasional "boost."

The fact is, you can reach thousands of your followers and even some new targets for very little investment by boosting your posts via paid ads against specific targets. The costs are far less than what it used to cost nonprofits to reach their audiences by direct mail. In a way, social media platforms have learned a few things from the U.S. Postal Service (charging you to reach your own list), but they do it more efficiently and supply you with reports and statistics unmatched by older "analog" methods.

I'm not recommending you boost every post, but the release of a new video, an event, or a matching gift opportunity are the kinds of posts that deserve to be seen and maximized.

One "free" way to boost your posts is to do so on public social group pages that provide group-generated town news and happenings. Don't be annoying by overdoing it, and keep the "big three" (quantity, quality, and variety) top of mind as you pursue this strategy, but such activity is a great way to boost your content awareness and grow your following.

Ask Yourself a Few Tough Questions

As you look at your social media possibilities and efforts, it's good to be constantly asking yourself some tough questions. Those include:

- How many social platforms can you really manage well (considering your time, resource, and talent constraints)?
- Does your organization have the right skills and resources to serve particular platforms? (Keep in mind that most platforms need eye-catching graphics or photography as well as decent video production and editing.)
- What platforms are your competitors or similar organizations using (even those in other communities)? Remember, you can set up social media monitoring alerts using inexpensive online tools to track any organization's content and activity, which can help you determine where you should be and even inspire your own content.

- What platforms are delivering the most engagement from the demographic you're targeting? (This information may provide you an answer for where to put your time and resources.)
- What type of content drives the best engagement on each platform? (This can give insight into the type of new content to create.)

The medium *is* the message.

After spending a good portion of this chapter devaluing and discounting traditional media, I'm now going to turn the tables a bit and tell you why it's still important to consider strategies to engage with them via advertising or public relations efforts.

Despite all the hype on use and accessibility of social media, traditional media is still very much a force. It's not only still used as much as any vehicle (see the following chart), but it also is consumed as much as any other content.

Despite its decline in use, traditional media content is still consumed (sometimes on newer, more mobile devices) as much as it ever was. Some would argue that through delayed viewing and social sharing, it's now consumed more than ever before!

Beyond these statistics and numbers, there's also the credibility factor—the perception that when you're interviewed or seen on traditional media channels, it is more legitimate or has higher value than being seen or heard on a podcast or within the newsfeed of any social channel.

In a recent presentation on this topic, I asked people in the audience to see being on television as the "Carnegie Hall" of media. Being heard on radio is like sharing the airwaves with the U.S. Navy "Blue Angels" flight team. And being on an outdoor billboard is like being seen on a giant movie screen.

CHANGING MEDIA CONSUMPTION

In a single decade, the way in which we consume media has shifted dramatically. Everyday
mobile use has skyrocketed, underscoring the move away from offline media.

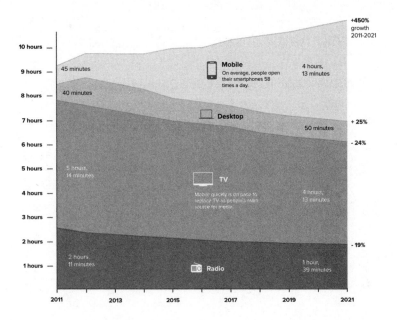

Communication theorist Marshall McLuhan coined the phrase,
"The medium is the message." He said that the medium itself shapes
and controls "the scale and form of human association and action."[41]

Basically, McLuhan was conveying that there is a greater
emotional response to being seen or featured on some media that
is unrivaled by other platforms. My point here is, even today, traditional media still carries more weight and "wow" factor than social
platforms. So don't ignore it!

Can you now see your organization as a powerful media vehicle,
thought leader, and champion for the cause you've taken on? Are
you ready to "pick up the megaphone" and become a stronger and
more effective voice for those people and things that need your help?
If so, I invite you to use and maximize these tips to do more good for
you . . . and for them.

CHAPTER 35

PR Support: Why My Public Relations Friends Hate Me (and Other Interesting PR Tidbits)

Public relations practitioners are very savvy people. They're strategic. They're good writers. They're objective. They construct good arguments. They have nerves of steel. They speak well, and, generally, they present themselves well.

But they *do* have a "kryptonite," and that is being labeled as part of the marketing mix. I dare you to say to any serious PR practitioner that they're just another cog in the marketing wheel, especially a PR pro who is Accredited in Public Relations (APR designation after their name). You'll see their eyes roll, shoulders drop, and faces contort as menacingly as a teenaged girl listening to "dad jokes" from her father.

I get it; there is a part of their job known as crisis management and putting together a plan and managing a crisis take Woodward and Bernstein brains and Erin Brockovich bravery. Because of that aspect of their profession, PR practitioners have removed themselves from the marketing mix and claim they should be sitting at the top executive decision-making table with the CEO, CFO, and the CMO. They believe they should report directly to their organization's president!

Essentially, they want to be treated and respected as substantive advisors on par with an attorney or a CPA, and not just seen as a "tool" of marketing.

Admittedly, I have extra sensitivity to the concerns of PR practitioners because I once worked with and for Pat Jackson, whom some argue belongs on a PR Mount Rushmore along with the "Father of PR," Edward Bernays. [42] Looking back on that experience, I'm somewhat perplexed about why Pat even bothered to discuss this topic with me, let alone put up with my arguments about why PR belongs in a marketing plan and shouldn't be seen as a completely separate discipline.

The fact of the matter is, most reputable business schools teach that, indeed, PR is an expertise and tactical element that exists within one of the 4 Ps of marketing and, specifically, in the "P" known as "Promotion." (All my PR friends just dropped their shoulders, rolled their eyes, contorted their faces, and likely threw another dart at the cover of this book attached to their dartboard.)

Promotion! The PR practitioner would object like an unacceptable motion from an opposing attorney in court. However, from a more objective point of view, it's easy to say that, even in a crisis, the ultimate goal of a PR professional is to protect the organization and its brand. So even in a PR manager's toughest moment, they're not only called on to do and say the right thing, their success will include salvaging the organization's reputation so that it can continue to do the good it is known for doing.

Maybe that's too much "inside baseball" jargon for many, but there is a difference of opinion between many PR practitioners and CEOs as to what is, in fact, "good PR." Most CEOs, because they're trained in business and management schools, understand that good PR means getting publicity or "buzz" that creates and results in media coverage. In short, CEOs want their brands promoted, and any crisis that may arise managed in ways that will protect the brand.

Earned. Owned. Paid.

In the previous chapter I talked a lot about media, mostly related to owned and paid opportunities. Just so we're on the same page, here's a quick clarification of these terms:

Owned Media | Websites, blogs, vlogs, newsletters, podcasts, and social media pages that are managed, developed, and curated by an organization.

Paid Media | Advertising on websites, search engines, and all social/digital media platforms (also on all traditional media channels such as TV, radio, print, and outdoor).

Earned Media | Stories, features, segments, interviews, speaking engagements, and mentions by, with, or for third parties in traditional and digital media channels, as well as public and private events that are cultivated through efforts and relations spearheaded by the communication and PR team.

With all that in mind, this chapter is about *earned* media and how best to manage and secure it. And despite having a little fun in my introduction at the expense of PR practitioners, I can tell you that they are worth their weight in gold.

After all, in this day when even bad PR can be good, a bad reputation or bad press can be disastrous for a nonprofit organization. So my first tip—above all others—would be to hire a pro and listen to their counsel.

Nine Good Tips to Get Good PR

That said, here are some more tips for getting good PR:

1. **Don't wait to be called.**

   Good story opportunities don't typically get noticed on their own, especially today when media outlets are overwhelmed with press releases and budget cuts are leaving them with smaller and smaller staffs. So connect with journalists and media contacts on a personal level with a tip or idea via email or by phone.

2. **Media wants to be served, not sold.**

   Instead of sending a press release, write to a media contact with your idea and why it works for their audience, then ask for permission to send a release. Keep in mind that a media outlet wants to be involved in putting a story together that resonates with their audience, not told what you desire or want them to do.

3. **Media covers stories, not just facts and figures.**

   Work hard to communicate your stories to the media in ways that capture their hearts and emotions. It's usually best to start with a personal or impact story instead of facts and figures. The more interesting and extraordinary you make the elements of your story, the more you'll increase its appeal and newsworthiness.

4. **Make news, not news releases.**

   There are times when you have urgent or breaking news that is worthy of immediate attention. That's when you need to stick to a "just the facts" approach. But you *must* already have good media relationships in place and have built trust with media contacts for your important news item to break through and quickly get into the news cycle. If you don't have that, it is always smart to work with a professional who does.

5. **Friend a media friend.**

Simple as this sounds, if you "friend" and follow media contacts on social media, you'll be surprised how accessible they are. It also doesn't hurt to be the kind of friend who "likes" and "comments" on their posts. Don't overdo this; that can be annoying, not to mention unprofessional. And don't pitch your stories to media personalities via their social media channels. If you don't already have their email address, you can ask them via private messaging what is the best email to submit story ideas for them to consider.

6. **Be a student and ask questions.**

Monitor media channels that you know you'll want to pitch. Study what they cover and how they like to report things. Adapt your pitches and stories to their specific styles, and even connect your story to similar ones you've seen that have gotten good engagement on their own platforms in the past. Also, don't be afraid to ask media contacts questions. Getting them to mentor and educate you about what they like to see or cover is a great way to build a relationship and demonstrate your desire to *serve* them (not *sell* them!).

7. **Preach to the choir and call choir practice.**

Tip #2 (that media wants to be served, not sold) is a Pat Jackson classic. This tip is from his "greatest hits" album of advice, as well. His point is that so much of media relations is about getting covered, and not enough attention is given to being *prepared* to be covered. That means, when reporters show up expectedly or unexpectedly, you and your organization need to be ready for them. Chances are, the media won't want to talk to just the PR person when building their story, so a number of people in your organization will need to be prepared, trained, and ready to respond to potential questions. This is especially true in a crisis where "no comment" is the equivalent of "guilty as charged" in the world of managing perceptions.

8. **Make your website media-friendly.**

This tip and the next one come from a contributing author within domoregood.org's Cause Network.[43] Once a reporter or blogger knows about you, the first thing they hit is your website. Set up a media or press room on your site, stocked with news releases, fact sheets, and free-to-use photos and videos. Include links to media stories that have covered your organization. Provide good contact information, including email addresses and phone numbers of people whom reporters can contact immediately. Respond right away to any interest by any media anywhere. Writers, bloggers, and reporters work on deadlines. If you don't respond right away, they will find another organization willing to work with them.

9. **Start small.**

Also from Cause Network is this tip: A small story, even an announcement about your special event or volunteer project in a weekly publication, could lead to interest from the local TV station. A local TV story could lead to its affiliate network's interest. A story on the local NPR station could lead to a national feature. Frequent and consistent contact with local media raises the odds of getting some great exposure. (Hmmm ... frequency wins; that's an interesting idea!)

Is your organization truly working to acquire *earned* media opportunities? Do you have the team members who could lead these important brand-building and awareness efforts? If it can't be done internally, my experience has been that there are many smart and cost-conscious PR professionals in every market who can consult and help your organization get more media attention ... so you can do *more* good.

Next let's look at what kind of "Success" you could generate if you implement each step of the IDEAS Process.

PART VI

SUCCESS

IDEAS PROCESS
S = Success

"Nothing motivates like success." I really believe that. But often success takes some trial and error. In fact, I've only seen a handful of great ways to generate success right from the start of a new initiative.

One of my clients has now perfected this. Every year this client launches a new media program to influence specific target audiences and improve outcomes. And each year at their annual banquet, which happens to be the biggest nonprofit banquet in our state, they premiere their new media campaign to their donors as a sneak-peak before they see it on TV or within their social media newsfeeds.

My client then asks the banquet guests for the funds to purchase airtime and media space for this campaign. Since they've seen the emotionally compelling video ads, the guests can imagine the impact they'll have, and they are very inclined to give generously.

This same client used to rely on high-paid speakers, celebrities, and musicians who would be flown in to host the evening or entertain their donors. Many times, they spent so much money on these performers that it was hard to realize a good ROI on the event.

My client discovered that asking donors to join a specific cause and showing them exactly what they'd be supporting was their best path to success. They learned that it is better, and more effective, for people not just to hear about your plans and strategy, but to *feel* them as well.

CHAPTER 36

Valuable Partnerships: ROI of the Third Kind

Even Greater ROI Happens when Businesses and Nonprofits Partner

As you know by now, I fervently advocate that nonprofits take a page from the playbook of successful for-profit brands to view dollars spent on marketing as an *investment,* not as an *expense.* It's a simple principle—smart and sustained investments in your brand will lead to growth. When you grow, you can do *more* good.

Today we're seeing a reverse trend—a new breed of for-profit businesses is now ripping a page from the nonprofit playbook! These businesses are working for more than a return on investment, they also desire to make an *impact on* the world around them. Their concept is built on this simple premise: It's good business to grow your business for the greater good. Many of these new businesses are really hybrids of the for-profit and nonprofit worlds—enterprises that integrate social and environmental objectives with business practices. They've created the emerging category of "for-benefit" enterprise, and they're driving what's being called an *Impact Economy.*

A Madcap Scheme

In his blog post for *U.S. News & World Report*, cofounder and board of directors member of The American Sustainable Business Council, David Brodwin, profiles Grand Rapids, Michigan-based Madcap Coffee Company as exemplary among emerging for-benefit enterprises.

From their "Zero Waste" policy, to their established practice of working directly with coffee growers to improve crop quality, harvesting, and processing techniques, Madcap Coffee is committed to socially responsible business practices that benefit both their local community and global suppliers. The result is a higher-quality product that Madcap commits to buy directly from the farmers at a higher price. Customers get a better product, farmers get a better price, and the community gets a strong local business and an environmentally conscious neighbor.[44]

Peter Drucker wrote about this in a *Harvard Business Review* article titled, "What Business Can Learn from Nonprofits." In that piece, he wrote: "Nonprofits don't base their strategy on money...they focus on performance of mission."[45]

That means a focus on good mission and good performance can also lead to good financial returns.

"Good" Business

What's different about this new business trend is that "good" is now a strategic advantage, not just a philanthropic gesture—one that can be leveraged to draw supporters and grow both nonprofits and businesses, large and small.

While Amway, Inc. might not fit everyone's definition of a "for-benefit" enterprise, the credo of Amway cofounder Rich DeVos, whose book is titled *Compassionate Capitalism,* has been recognized by many as the forefront of this movement.[46] John Mackey, co-CEO of Whole Foods, updated that philosophy in his

2013 release *Conscious Capitalism* by challenging businesses to be about creating value, not only for investors, but also for customers, employees, suppliers, local communities, and the environment.[47]

And consider this from organizers of a Harvard University summit that brought together powerhouses as diverse as Deutsche Bank, GlaxoSmithKline, Goodwill Industries International, Harvard School of Business, U.S. Departments of Commerce and Treasury, and the EPA to discuss growing the impact economy:

"For-benefit enterprises . . . create quality jobs and promote economic growth, contribute to the tax base, drive new resources to the nonprofit sector, and tackle a wide range of social and environmental issues that would otherwise fall on the shoulders of government and nonprofits. These enterprises are drivers of an 'impact economy'—one that promotes social, environmental, and economic value creation."[48]

Now that's "good" business. And it has serious implications for the nonprofit world.

Leveraging Your—and Their—Driving Purpose

Like their nonprofit counterparts, these socially conscious businesses have been built on a driving purpose—a purpose that truly matters and is at the heart of what makes them thrive.

But don't be fooled. These more socially conscious businesses aren't simply motivated by doing good—they also know such practices are good for business.

"Consumers are looking for a new type of relationship with brands and purpose is really central to that," said Cécile Nathan-Tilloy, managing director and primary research lead at Edelman Europe.[49]

In a recent global consumer study done by Edelman, Nathan-Tilloy highlighted that "90% of consumers say that by supporting the brands they love; they feel like they are actively supporting the cause that the brand is behind."[50]

Nonprofits need to be aware of this trend, study the for-benefit enterprises that are driven by a similar purpose as their own, and get creative in proposals to partner with these businesses for increased ROI.

Win-Win-Win

One approach I advocate to getting "good" businesses to partner with and support your organization (and maybe, even underwrite your marketing efforts) is to position the opportunity to do so as a "win-win-win" proposition.

So often in business partnerships, the goal is to create a "win-win" situation. What's unique to partnering with a nonprofit is that there is a third win opportunity available. I call this concept "ROI of the Third Kind."

At this point when I'm speaking on this topic, I know there are people sitting in the audience who expect actor Richard Dreyfuss and a bunch of aliens from Mars to come out and invade my presentation.[51] But really, this concept is not otherworldly, and it's not difficult to understand or implement.

The Three ROIs Are

Return On Investment—It's leverageable for the good of business and nonprofit through good public relations, greater awareness and interest, increased business and giving, and better perceptions related to philanthropy and success.

Return On Involvement—It's engaging good done and then felt by the employees, customers, vendors, and shareholders (e.g., many of those audiences can be asked to participate in the good being done and the resulting joy is spread to many people connected to one or both organizations).

Return On Impact—It's measurably good in helping the people, things, or cause in need.

The key is knowing how to use this concept to "sell" a for-profit business on the feasibility of partnering with your organization so that they see that the ROI makes sense . . . and makes good business sense as well.

The author of *Storytelling in the Digital Age: A Guide for Nonprofits*, Julia Campbell, offers some advice about how to find a business to partner with: "Tell a story that will resonate with a particular business partner," she says. "Find out what they have invested in previously, where their interests lie, and what other organizations they are involved with."[52] This doesn't have to require a lot of upfront work; simply search a business's website and look at the "About" and "Mission" pages. This will quickly tell you whether its values align with your own.

Be Sure to Choose a "Good" Partner

When reaching out to companies of any size, nonprofits can highlight how they are:

- Aligned with the business's values
- Able to help boost sales, visibility, and employee or consumer loyalty
- Positioned to strengthen the business's reputation

Focusing on businesses that a) are strongly aligned with your values, b) appeal to the community you serve or your donors, and c) both connect with the right people and have strong reputations will help exponentially with your outreach.[53]

An example of a good partnership is between American Express and The National Trust for Historic Preservation, which work together to back historic small restaurants. American Express cards are used frequently at restaurants and historic destinations, so maintaining a good reputation in those industry segments is just good business in addition to being a good cause match. Another naturally synergistic partnership exists between Uber Eats and the No Kid Hungry initiative, and between the partnership of Pottery Barn and the national Arbor Day Foundation. All these partnerships

bring needed awareness and support to nonprofits and their beneficiaries; plus, they enhance the image of a corporate entity in a way
that dovetails well with its image and its product or service offering.

Beyond the basics of what makes a good nonprofit partner, a
few other best practices for selecting and launching a partnering
program include:

- **Choose carefully**—Don't just pick a partner based on public
  relations and financial opportunities. Make sure both the
  business and the nonprofit looking to partner see this as a
  lasting and mutually beneficial effort.
- **Choose relevance**—Be sure the partnership makes sense
  not just to the organizations involved but for all who come
  in contact with both the business and nonprofit. A beer
  company supporting substance abuse or a candymaker partnering to fight obesity are just two examples of partnerships
  that may cause more concerns than growth!
- **Start a movement**—If everyone seems to be solely interested in a campaign, maybe it's not an ideal partnership. It's
  better to partner with a business that wants to contribute
  to the conversation of making things holistically better and
  not just looking to help to lift giving proceeds and public
  awareness for a quarter.
- **Secure involvement**—To be great partners, both the business and the nonprofit should be responsive to each other's
  needs and act on a sense of responsibility toward creating
  success for each other. Self-centered, one-way perspectives
  and programs are the antithesis of partnering for good.

Hopefully all this sheds new light on the opportunities within
business and nonprofit partnerships and gives you and your organization a new perspective on the potential (triple) returns from these
relationships!

Some Challenging Questions to Ask Yourself and Your Organization

- Can our nonprofit organization offer partnerships relevant to the societal or environmental concerns that drive these new for-benefit enterprises?
- Can we help leaders of these for-profit organizations grow their impact by tapping them for board or committee positions?
- Can we build a fundraising or friend-raising program around our common purpose that also drives customer and donor engagement and loyalty for their organization and ours?
- Can we help these businesses leverage their driving purpose for greater impact and returns?

Think about it. Then start sharing your ideas with potential business partners so everyone can grow from them. We'll next take a look at what success looks like when our goals are measurable.

CHAPTER 37

Measuring Performance: Start with the Last Step in Mind

Stephen Covey's book *The 7 Habits of Highly Effective People* has made a huge impact on my professional thinking—even though I've never really read the whole book. I say that sheepishly since there have been many great books that have been given to me and recommended in such a way by friends that I get the important highlights (in CliffNotes fashion), without having to read the whole book.

It's awesome when a highly effective person has already done the work of reading a book and tells me the top two or three points that I can immediately put into practice!

That's the case with this book. A trusted business advisor I know handed it to me and said, "There's a lot of great stuff in here, but 'Begin with the End in Mind' [Habit #2] is extremely good advice." My friend went on to explain that this concept centered around an exercise of writing your own or your organization's obituary. By doing so, you end up writing an inspirational story about what you ultimately want to achieve (individually or organizationally). From there, you'll have set a powerful vision and articulated your goals, and you can then begin planning accordingly.

To that end, when it comes to planning for campaign or marketing or branding success, I always encourage organizations I work with to tell me first what "success" will look like to them. Once we do that, our planning and strategizing will be centered on achieving the success and outcomes we define at the outset.

Nothing Motivates Like Success

Again and again, program after program, organization after organization, I've seen firsthand how motivating success can be. Especially when success goes beyond just financial returns and a vision is cast to achieve something big, audacious, and inspirational. Without a doubt, financial success needs to be one of the measures of success (remember from chapter 2, "No margin. No mission."), but I've seen too many times when success is overly, or even solely, focused upon financial outcomes...and those measures provide diminishing returns.

This is where true leadership enters the picture, and bold visionaries need to define success clearly, with a level of inspiration that is not only motivating but leaves people feeling like they are involved in doing something heroic.

The nonprofit world, which naturally puts mission ahead of margin, is a place where success and rewards can deliver very rich and rewarding experiences for those who participate. After all, when a nonprofit organization succeeds, then lives, things, and circumstances are changed for good.

What Does Success Look Like for You?

This question is one of my favorites to ask someone or a group of people in charge of managing an organization. It's also a place I find a lot of humility in that I realize that I'm not a dreammaker; instead, as a communications expert, I'm simply an interpreter of dreams. If I'm going to be part of any success, it depends on understanding the best possible outcomes we hope to achieve upfront, so that I will spend little to no time on things that don't really matter.

Some of the more inspirational and often unarticulated measures of success include:

- Impact made
- Change created
- Life-altering things delivered/distributed
- People/animals/things helped (or saved)
- Bad things eliminated or eradicated
- Minds/hearts reached
- Transformational outcomes
- Care/comfort/peace provided
- Growth/achievement made possible
- New and better alternatives brought to light
- Fun or enlightenment or inspiration created
- Horizons expanded

I'm sure you could add many more measures of success to this list; such "hope" metrics make achieving everything else that follows worth the effort.

Key Performance Indicators (KPIs)

Maybe you've heard of the term "blocking and tackling." In American football, those are two of the most basic skills for the game. They are the least glamorous positions but are critically important to the team as a whole.

"Blocking and tackling" success points typically center around extremely measurable (and predictable) items such as:

- Revenue, donation levels, or growth
- Event attendance
- Volunteer signups

- **Web traffic and engagement** (visitors, sessions, unique visitors, page views, time spent on site, bounce rates, and so forth)
- **Follower growth, retention, and shares** (regarding social media following and engagement)
- **Clicks on social media posts/ads** (click-through rate, conversions, cost per impression (CPI), cost per click (CPC))
- **E-effort performance** (delivery rate, unsubscribe rate, open rate, forwards/shares)
- **Content engagement** (blog, vlog, newsletter reads, comments, likes, forwards/shares)
- **Return on ad spend (ROAS), Return on marketing investment (ROMI)**
- **Total engagement** (web traffic + social clicks + event attendance + volunteer activity + donations + and so on)

Other success measurables are evaluation indicators to help accomplish some of the more standard measures of success just listed. Those include:

- **Cost-per-visitor** (on the web or even for in-person events)
- **Web-to-lead conversions** (used to measure leads generated initially by the web; this could be used for any tactic, and tactic efficiency could then be compared. For instance, event-to-lead, direct-mail-to-lead, PR placement-to-lead, and so forth)
- **Lead-to-donation conversion rate** (per the preceding, this can be used to measure any tactic and compare the efficiency of any leading tactic that leads to donations)
- **Lifetime value** (some, if not all, tactics take time to prove their efficiency so tracking leads and donation for an extended period will give you a more complete picture of efficiency and effectiveness)

Not-So-Soft Measures of Success

Speaking of lifetime value, there are more measures of success that contribute significantly to overall performance and success, but they are harder to benchmark and track. Many CEOs tend to think of these as "soft" measurables, but the reality is, they are big contributors, often from the top of the sales funnel, which generate significant and needed momentum more than specific outcomes. These include:

- **Awareness created**
- **Impressions made**
- **Perceptions created and changed**
- **Market share increases** (percentage of giving in a category or geographic area)
- **Mindshare growth** (awareness + impressions in a category or geographic area)

The end, but really a new beginning.

Obviously this is not meant to be an exhaustive list of everything that can be measured, nor is it meant to provide a definition of what all these measurements mean (there are plenty of other great resources to dive further into this kind of information). But this should help get you started in your thinking about the many different ways to measure success. And the good news: There are many inexpensive tracking tools available to help you understand and report these figures accurately and efficiently.

What's important, though, is where I began. That is, you really need to know your endgame before you start. Because if you don't, even a slight deviation from an unexpressed or undefined beginning goal can lead you very far off track in the end. Then you won't likely do all the good you intended—you'll actually do less good. And nobody wants that.

CHAPTER 38

Sustaining Success: Stop Majoring in the Minors

Often when I meet with nonprofit leaders and communicators for the first time, we explore their organization's past successes and failures. Following are some of the common "success" answers I get during such dialogues. Note: I'm leaving out the last word that's almost always used when they provide one of these answers:

- We had this event...
- We got this news story...
- We did this outing...
- We held this dinner...
- We hosted this speaker...
- We orchestrated a series...
- We put on this concert...
- We ran this campaign...

As I noted in an earlier chapter, nearly every one of these stories or statements typically ends with the same word—and that word is "once."

Once Upon a Time Is Only Good for Fairytales

I told you that the five words I hate the most are, "We're the best-kept secret." Well, you can now add the word "once" to that list of words I hate. Once-upon-a-time moments, events, and situations are great for fairytales, but they're awful for organizations that want to create and sustain success.

Should your organization take advantage of once-in-a-lifetime opportunities as they present themselves? Absolutely. Ideally, though, you'll figure out how to leverage even those opportunities to help build momentum for and action behind other, sustainable activities, as well.

When you have a once-in-a-lifetime speaker, event, or story, you must make sure you take advantage of those moments and that swell of attention to create something that will last—maybe build volunteer signups or grow email lists or increase followers on social platforms. Just don't let that "once in a lifetime" go to waste.

You don't have to do it in the moment—you can leverage such incidents for months, even years afterward. You can continue to refer to these moments in press releases, direct mail, and social media. For instance, "We're the organization you read about ... or heard an A-list celebrity mention ... or we put on that concert with the big act that came to town." You can turn "once" into many, *many* opportunities to grow your awareness, credibility, following, and fan base.

Control the Controllables

Another way organizations "major in the minors" is they put a lot of effort, stock, and message execution in the control of others. Either through third-party channels such as the media and PR efforts, organic web search efforts, social media likes and shares, or volunteer and board of directors' networks, too many nonprofits depend too much on others to carry, craft, share, and convey their messaging to the world.

Passive efforts have value, especially third-party endorsements. But proactive efforts such as marketing, advertising, mailing, e-mailing, and (boosted) social media postings give you much-needed control, consistency, continuity, and sustainability. Even proactively managing your passive efforts is an opportunity to control your messaging.

As I pointed out in chapter 35 on PR, your organization needs to preach to the choir and have choir practice—which means many tools should be developed and training mandated for staff, leadership, volunteers, consultants, and board members, basically, anyone who comes in contact with your brand on a professional or volunteer basis. They are all opinion leaders for your organization, and they all need to communicate consistently and constantly about your organization. Leaving those opportunities to chance and not maximizing them to your organization's benefit is not just unfortunate, it's irresponsible!

After all, as I've said previously, there are only three possible outcomes of any brand contact: positive, negative, or unrealized. And unrealized (those that make no lasting impression or are not maximized) are by far worse than negative! Control your messaging by taking ownership and leveraging every possible opportunity to advance your brand and the good you want to achieve.

Putting a Ten-Pound Bag Against a Ten-Pound Problem

I had a business client who was a significant philanthropist. When he supported a nonprofit organization, he always looked for organizational excellence and the ability to manage problems and opportunities efficiently. Some of his wisdom came, obviously, from his success in business. But I learned over time that his military service on the battlefields in Vietnam also gave him incredible insights. He learned in the trenches what it took to work and succeed under pressure. It took me a while to understand one of his oft-used expressions, but I soon realized that it's great advice.

This Vietnam vet turned successful businessman and amazing philanthropist would say about the need to manage situations well: "They just need to learn to put a ten-pound bag against a ten-pound problem."

When I heard him say this, I thought he was observing that there was too much or too little effort or action related to a specific opportunity or problem. Eventually I began to appreciate that it also meant to make sure you're proactively prioritizing all your resources appropriately, assuring that you're putting forth the right amount of organizational effort and weight to provide the greatest protection or return.

I'll admit, I was slow to also comprehend that he was literally talking about sandbags, which are filled and placed against an oncoming issue or problem that demands a sense of urgency, many times because it was unexpected.

Of course, never having served in the military myself, I imagined at first that he was referring to the kind of small sandbags used to protect a property or area against flooding. But in the case of my vet-turned-philanthropic friend, he was talking about the kind of huge sandbags used to protect you and your troops from oncoming bullets.

Efficiency, appropriate measures, and readiness take on new meaning when your life is on the line! Such things move from being just good efforts to being necessary for your survival!

This concept applies to all organizations, but especially those that are scrappy, small, and struggling. Chances are, if you're one of those organizations, you have limited resources, few staff members, little time, and you may feel as if you're dodging bullets constantly.

That's all the more reason not to waste resources or time by putting too much of your effort against problems and opportunities that can be managed by less time and fewer resources.

Do Good, Better

Places where I often see organizations fail to allocate time and resources well are in efforts such as social media, events, and trying to get agencies, consultants, and media to give them free time and service.

When I first started advising nonprofits as a business, it was hard not to want to give away my time and my agency's time pro bono. But the fact was and is, I couldn't keep my own lights on and qualified staff members onboard if I did. When I was able to provide services for free, I could only do it for an organization once; therefore, it wouldn't be a sustainable effort. Immediate needs and satisfaction would be exchanged for long-term returns and impact.

In social media, I see organizations invest incredible amounts of time and effort only to get a few "likes," virtually no "shares," and very small returns. Events, such as banquets, lunches, golf outings, and auctions, are probably where I see the greatest inefficiencies among the nonprofits I've served. I often hear how much is raised at an event, but I almost never hear how much it truly cost in planning time, effort, salaries, and other resources allocated. Beyond that, I've never had an organization I've worked with do a true analysis of whether raising those resources could have been done more efficiently in another way ... perhaps for even greater returns.

Does that mean you should stop doing such efforts? No, but it does mean you should put the right amount of resources and weight against those efforts for the return you're getting.

It's Still the Art of Persuasion

It's no secret—I'm a marketing guy. I believe marketing works (and there is plenty of evidence that it does, especially within the consumer and business marketplaces), but I also know that one of the key objectives of marketing is to lower the cost of selling. If your marketing isn't getting more efficient over time (six- to eighteen-month measurements of effort is standard) or if it's not providing a greater return on your investment, then it's not that marketing doesn't work—it's that your marketing program isn't working!

Successful marketing programs require practice and precision. They need to hit the right people at the right time with the right message. Sometimes everything comes together flawlessly; most often, things just need to be tweaked and twisted into shape. As much science as we try to apply to it, marketing is still mostly about the "art of persuasion."

So if you're not constantly looking to prioritize your marketing and communication efforts appropriately, putting the right amount of effort toward a specific problem or opportunity, then you're not being a good steward. In fact, you're potentially jeopardizing the life and lifeblood of your organization—the margin needed to help advance and grow your mission!

Majoring in the minors, telling yourself fairytales, not controlling what's controllable, and managing growth resources poorly is not a plan to do *more* good. How badly do you want to do good? Hopefully, badly enough to stop, measure, think, and change for good.

So now you're ready to ask yourself, *What if I could only do one thing?*

CHAPTER 39

A Success Secret: If I Could Do Only One Thing

With more than thirty years of experience, working for and with some of the world's biggest and most successful brands, and giving hundreds of speeches and presentations to nonprofit organization gatherings, I'm frequently asked what is the single most impactful thing that nonprofits can do to help make their marketing communications program more successful.

While I'm always quick to say there is no "magic bullet" when it comes to marketing and branding success, knowing that an integrated and coordinated mix of program elements is always best, there is one strategy that, if I were a betting man, I would place my money on time and time again: **frequency.**

Obviously, frequency works best when it's targeting the right audience, has well-honed messaging, breakthrough creative, and features a strong call to action. But for the most part, frequency can be successful without many of the elements that are considered "pivotal" by marketing and branding experts.

Frequency comes in many shapes and sizes. Apple **frequently innovates** and makes frequent splashes to tell us of their latest and greatest innovation. McDonald's wins by using frequency too—they're **frequently accessible** (with convenient locations, hours, service, menu choices, prices, and so forth) and they advertise their accessibility . . . very frequently.

Frequency is a key element in Nike's brand success, as well. While they've certainly been a frequent advertiser in the past, Nike today relies heavily on the strategy of **frequent prevalence**. They are so ubiquitous in sports that almost any uniform, piece of equipment, or ball looks incomplete without the Nike "swoosh" visible on it—in high school games and matches, as well as in the professional leagues!

Frequency Wins for Nonprofits Too

Whether you realize it or not, one thing that almost every top brand name, celebrity, cause, and even every politician has in common is that they employ a frequency strategy. That doesn't mean just frequent advertising; it's doing any one thing, communication-wise, repeatedly and frequently.

World Vision does one main thing frequently—child sponsorship. Even though its strategy may seem like a one-trick pony, it's done it frequently enough that it's one of the top ten nonprofit organizations in the U.S.

What its child sponsorship model does well frequently is create **engagement**—the child writes to their donor for their monthly support; it's personal and touching—and some of its donors have become so engaged that they travel across the globe to meet this child they've supported.

World Vision's program has respect—and many others have tried to imitate it. It has stayed with that model—and that's its recipe for success: frequency.

Habitat for Humanity doesn't just ask for donations, it gets people swinging a hammer—that's frequency of **involvement**. Each person it engages to swing a hammer at one of its homesites is going to tell dozens of other people about their experience, which then motivates others not only to donate but also to get involved. Frequency wins for Habitat for Humanity and it's found a great formula that's worth repeating!

The Salvation Army, with its red buckets and bellringers, also uses the principle of frequency with frequent **presence**. And it's used this to become one of the top nonprofit brands in the nation. Beyond that, it's used frequency to overcome a potential barrier that many other faith-based organizations can't seem to overcome. That barrier is a potentially niche and even divisive name. Interestingly, as overt as its name is, which communicates it's a Christian organization looking to convert people and is fairly militant in its actions, it's so often seen as doing good that hardly anyone associates its name with high-pressure religious conversion efforts.

Howard Schultz, the founder of Starbucks, understands the concept of frequency as well as anyone. As I mentioned in an earlier chapter, he was once asked, "What is branding? And Schultz responded, "Understanding branding is easy . . . *everything matters.*"

Which means that everything Starbucks does is intentionally on-brand and executed to the highest degree of excellence possible. When you walk into a Starbucks and everything is supremely well-designed—the music, the fixtures, the packaging, the food, the signage, the menu, the baristas, the aromas—it's simply a very well-orchestrated brand that understands that everything, indeed, matters.

What Schultz has learned is you don't even need to advertise frequently if you are doing **everything** frequently well!

I attended an event and heard this story that Schultz was at a gathering in a brand-new Starbucks opening in a major city. This location was being touted to be one of their marquee stores, a store of the future, and in the midst of all the fanfare with the event going on and the press all around, Schultz was sitting quietly looking out the front window. A reporter came up to him and said, "This store is fantastic! But why are you staring across the street. What are you looking at?"

Schultz said, "I'm thinking there needs to be another Starbucks across the street."

The reporter responded, "That's crazy! Another Starbucks across the street from this one?"

Schultz explained that this new store is strategically located for customers as they are on their way to work and having another location on the other side of the street would be convenient as people head home. It's a totally different vibe on that side of the street, he observed, and another Starbucks could be just as successful over there!

Now that's frequency of **exposure!**

To that end, what Schultz also understands is that a person walking around with a Starbucks cup in their hand is the equivalent of a television ad. Every Starbucks logo on a bag of coffee beans—that's a living commercial. And every one of their store locations is also like a billboard ad. They're not just coffee cups, coffee bags, or locations—they're all vivid and compelling ads! Starbucks employs frequency very well, and they win.

The satirical website The Onion posted a headline that read, "Starbucks Expansion Plan: New Starbucks Opening in the Bathrooms of Existing Starbucks." You can't go anywhere without running into a Starbucks or running into someone with a Starbucks logo on their cup, bag, or thermal mug. They're everywhere! And frequency is the key ingredient of their success.

Allow Me to Say This One More Time

Again, you can look at any successful organization, business, celebrity, politician, or cause and you will see something that they do repeatedly and well, something that they do with *frequency* that is a huge part of their success.

Watch for it ... learn from it ... and use it to win loyal followers. Engage raving fans and you will provide your organization with a sustainable advantage.

If you only recall one thing from this book, it needs to be this ...

Frequency wins.

CHAPTER 40

Conclusion:
Be a Brand, Not
an Organization

I was once asked to speak at a nonprofit leadership conference within a unique framework. The invitation required that any consultant presenting needed to conduct their presentation with the help of one of their clients. The conference organizers believed this would add a higher threshold of practicality to each presentation. Their perspective was that consultants tend to speak using broad concepts and don't reference enough relevant examples. They also explained that the leader-to-leader dynamic created from this model had been proven to improve the focus and usability of presentation content by those attending.

While I had certainly used many client examples in previous presentations, sharing the stage with a client presented some challenges, but it also presented an interesting opportunity. I had to determine which client I would ask, and it crossed my mind that other clients might be offended if they weren't chosen. There's also the reality that some people are just better presenters than others. Fortunately, the first client I asked accepted the invitation to be part of my presentation. He chose not to publicize this opportunity since he didn't think it would advance his organization's mission or his career (and that decision reduced the chance of my other clients finding out). In other words, I dodged a bullet by doing this presentation with one client, without upsetting the rest of my clients.

When preparing for this presentation, my client asked me to present the content I would normally prepare and then have him lead about 40 percent of the session. As such, he asked me to walk through the parts I wanted him to present so he could see it done as I would do it. He paid attention as I did the presentation for him, taking notes so he could add his own point of view and examples to the mix.

The presentation was titled, "10 Marketing Tips to Do More Good." It covered many practical tips, but it also required an overview of key marketing concepts to help nonprofits understand the role and importance of marketing for them. The audience at this conference was primarily made up of executive directors and CEOs, so it wasn't necessarily intuitive for them to understand how marketing and fundraising are different or how they could and should coexist.

After a lot of back and forth between my client and me while preparing for this presentation, my client said to me: "I think what you're trying to communicate is that a nonprofit needs to think of itself as a brand, not as an organization."

I didn't really expect this response, but it was brilliant. And it wasn't surprising, given my client's career path and background. His role at the time was serving a nonprofit with international reach having a profound impact on shaping families and culture. He had spent many years before this current role working in telecommunications and finance in Chicago and New York. I always appreciated working with him because he demanded my best thinking and seemed to know how to draw that out of me by asking great questions. Also, I appreciated that, like me, he had a lot of experience working with major brands so he understood what it took to become a name brand and how to maintain that status. I also liked that he gave up a successful career and money-making path by leaving corporate America so he could pursue an opportunity to do more good.

But when he said this statement: "Be a brand, not an organization," I was immediately struck with the fact that he essentially took everything I've been trying to say, teach, and preach, and he put it all into one very succinct phrase. Yet I needed to understand it through his eyes and from his experience. So I asked him, "What does 'Be a brand, not an organization mean to you?"

He replied, "When you look at the biggest and most successful companies in the world, they seem to understand something the nonprofit world doesn't really get—that is, they understand the importance and value of their brand."

At this point, I was the one taking notes and listening. And these are the thoughts I took down from my client.

Companies, institutions, and organizations that understand the importance and value of their brands do these things:

- See their brand as a series of "mental shortcuts" for important audiences to communicate what their company, institution, or organization does, what it does well, and what makes it unique and different.
- View their brand as their most important asset to be leveraged for success, growth, attention, partnerships, and investment.
- Recognize marketing as the fuel that grows their brand and, therefore, requires serious effort, risk-taking, and investment along with a measured and expected ROI.
- Look at their CEO as the person who needs to prioritize and spearhead leveraging and accelerating growth using marketing and innovation to increase brand recognition and value.
- Examine every decision and put it through a "brand filter" to determine whether it is "on brand" or not—that's true of hiring decisions, location decisions, technology decisions,

customer journey and support decisions, partnering decisions, board member decisions, giving and involvement
decisions, and sponsorship decisions.

"Basically, Bill," my client said to me as I was frantically writing
down his wisdom, "really successful companies cease to see themselves as companies, but instead, see themselves as brands. And
that's what creates uber success, growth, and gives them a sustainable advantage."

Then I asked, already knowing the answer, "And nonprofits don't
do this, do they?"

And my client said, "Sadly, no. And they limit the good they
could do as a result."

Though I had already been on my mission to help nonprofits to
do more good for well over fifteen years at this point, my client added
some "rocket fuel" to my quest. His insights (even though I was
supposed to be the one advising and teaching him) were profound.
They came from a life of experiences, perspectives, and education
that were much different than mine. Yet at the same time, we arrived
at much the same destination. The skills that had been used to sell
many things and helped create an often ugly, materialistic society
could be equally harnessed and used for good. But only if there were
good people to translate these concepts for the nonprofit community
and help these "ambassadors of good" execute them.

Marketing to become a brand and maintaining a brand's status
isn't a silver bullet to solve all organizational challenges, issues, and
problems, but I remember a boss who was known to use this simple
and motivating expression: "Revenue fixes a multitude of problems."
And there is no question—the business world knows that marketing
generates revenue. Even more so, there's not much doubt that the
nonprofit world could do a much better job competing for discretionary time and money by doing much better marketing.

If you're leading a nonprofit organization or leading its communication or fundraising efforts, I hope you'll appreciate that I have provided examples of many marketing concepts, principles, and practices in this book that will help your organization grow and maintain that growth.

Some of these key concepts include:

- Nonprofits are not the cause; they are a conduit to help a cause.
- Nonprofits have only one main purpose: to create a supporter.
- Without margin, nonprofits reduce the impact of their mission.
- The consumer market and businesses in general are the most formidable competitors for nonprofits when it comes to people's discretionary time and money.
- A nonprofit's voice in the marketplace competes with all other voices, especially those coming from the makers and marketers of consumer goods and services.
- Business and consumer marketers know they need an "air attack" (marketing) as well as a "ground attack" (personal selling) to be effective. Nonprofits need to also have an effective balance both of marketing and development efforts to achieve new levels of growth and sustainability.
- Nonprofits need to see marketing as an investment (that demands risk-taking and needs to provide a ROI) and not as an expense.
- Nonprofits must understand that an organization needs to market itself to become a brand.
- A brand is essentially a series of "mental shortcuts" for important audiences to understand what an organization does, what it does well, and what makes it unique.
- Branding encompasses many internal practices (staffing, delivery, meetings, interactions, training, identity,

leadership, and so on) as well as external efforts (marketing, advertising, fundraising, public relations, social media, and so forth).

- A method proposed in this book for developing and managing a successful and sustainable branding effort is to use the IDEAS Process, which is an acronym for Insights, Direction, Expression, Action, and Success:
  - Insights are gathered to establish a singular strategic vision that is unique, fact-based, relevant, and compelling.
  - Direction includes those things used to develop a strategic plan that will be executed and deployed through a variety of tactical efforts and media channels.
  - Expression is about bringing the brand messaging to life through creative exploration and final articulation.
  - Action is about executing strategies, directions, and expressions to bring it all to market and to audiences through various media, vehicles, channels, and platforms.
  - Success is about evaluating, optimizing, and growing opportunities and performance for the greatest impact.
- This IDEAS Process is a continuous improvement method and is not designed just for new efforts.
- Differentiation and messaging are both key to successful branding and marketing efforts, but don't overlook exposure (also known as frequency). Repetitive exposure is arguably the most important factor for successful institutions and organizations who achieve brand name status.
- Top-level success and impact are most always associated with an organization's ability to become a known brand.

With all that shared and said, I'd like to end this book the way I've ended many presentations over the past thirty years, and that is with a paraphrased quote from St. Maximus the Confessor:

"The knowledge of fire does not warm the body."[54]

So now that you have this knowledge, please go and do more good.

Acknowledgments

Katie Appold and Kathy Sindorf | Without your nudging, encouragement, and hard work, this book may have never been written.

(Retired) Professor Duane Schecter | Without your early encouragement and guidance, I'd be working in a factory and would have never pursued marketing/branding as an occupation or vocation.

Professor Dr. Charles Patti | Your standards and teaching methods set a bar I would work (and I am still working) to meet throughout my career.

Jim Hanon | Your faith, partnership, leadership, work ethic, and creativity have made doing more good a passion and reality in my work. Simply put, there would be no DO MORE GOOD without your influence and inspiration.

Will Oechsler, Jane Richtsmeier, and Jason Vanderground | Your strategic prowess and incredible desire to do good work for good things (not to mention your willingness to have fun and laugh in the process) have substantially shaped and influenced most of my methods, approaches, thinking, and content.

Mart Green, Barney Visser, and Rich DeVos | Your wisdom, passion for doing good, and incredible giving hearts have impacted so many, so often, for so long. I have been blessed to work for and with you, learning as much as I was doing—and most of all, being inspired by each of you to do good while staying focused on eternal outcomes.

All Hanon McKendry and HAVEN staff members | Every person I've worked with has made me better. Thank you for always challenging, pushing, sacrificing, creating, and thinking to make meaningful differences.

All Hanon McKendry and HAVEN clients | Whether for-profit or nonprofit, thank you for giving me the opportunities to help shape and work on your brands. These experiences have proven to be "the lab" where all DO MORE GOOD concepts and content were tried, applied, revised, and given a chance to thrive.

Compass College of Cinematic Arts, DoMoreGood.org, Nonprofit Hub, and Cause Camp | Various personnel, leadership, experiences, and events related to all these nonprofits have unquestionably impacted my work and my words.

American Advertising Federation (AAF) | Your workshops, awards competitions and events, clubs, members, content, and gatherings have helped shape me and my work. From being in the student advertising competition in college to being inducted into your Hall of Achievement, the AAF has been key to my professional development and practices.

Notes

1   Dr. Martin Luther King, Jr., "The Three Dimensions of a Complete Life," The Martin Luther King, Jr. Research and Education Institute, Stanford, accessed June 28, 2021, https://kinginstitute.stanford.edu/king-papers/publications/knock-midnight-inspiration-great-sermons-reverend-martin-luther-king-jr-6.

2   Chris Strub, *Forbes,* March 26, 2019, accessed June 29, 2021, https://www.forbes.com/sites/chrisstrub/2019/03/26/twitters-top-four-nonprofit-takeaways-from-2019-causethechange-cause-camp/?sh=22f420c28e26.

3   "Quotes by Archilochus," Goodreads, accessed June 30, 2021, https://www.goodreads.com/quotes/387614-we-don-t-rise-to-the-level-of-our-expectations-we.

4   Alice M. Tybout and Tim Calkins, editors; *Kellogg on Branding: The Marketing Faculty of The Kellogg School of Management,* Northwestern University (Wiley Publishing, 2016), 1.

5   William Cohen, "Only Two Basic Organizational Functions: Innovation and Marketing," HR Exchange Network, accessed June 23, 2021, https://www.hrexchangenetwork.com/hr-talent-management/columns/innovation-and-marketing.

6   Kim Schlossberg, "Branding for Non-profit Organizations: 11 Questions to Build Your Brand," LinkedIn, accessed June 28, 2021, https://www.linkedin.com/pulse/branding-non-profit-organizations-11-questions-build-your-kim/.

7   E. Jerome McCarthy, *Basic Marketing: A Managerial Approach* (Richard D. Irwin, Inc., 1960).

8   Jerome E. McCarthy, *Basic Marketing: A Managerial Approach* (Richard D. Irwin, Inc., 1960).

9   "The Circles of Marketing," Seth's Blog, accessed April 18, 2021, https://seths.blog/2012/07/the-circles-of-marketing/.

10 "Where Does Fundraising Begin?" The Agitator, accessed April 18, 2021, http://agitator.thedonorvoice.com/where-does-fundraising-begin/.

11 Ibid.

12 Christina Sterbenz, "12 Famous Quotes That Always Get Misattributed," *Business Insider,* Oct. 7, 2013, accessed July 5, 2021, https://www.businessinsider.com/misattributed-quotes-2013-10.

13 "Simon Sinek Quotes," AZQuotes.com, accessed June 22, 2021, https://www.azquotes.com/author/13643-Simon_Sinek.

14 Simon Sinek, *Start with Why* (Penguin Random House, 2009).

15 Simon Sinek TED Talk "Start with Why," YouTube, accessed June 21, 2021, https://youtu.be/_-fdJzvpX60.

16 "GEICO's 'Unskippable' from the Martin Agency is Ad Age's 2016 Campaign of the Year," *Ad Age,* accessed April 30, 2021, https://adage.com/article/special-report-agency-alist-2016/geico-s-unskippable-ad-age-s-2016-campaign-year/302300.

17 Anne-Christine Film Diaz, "Geico Nabs a Film Grand Prix at Cannes—With a Pre-Roll Ad," *Ad Age,* July 27, 2015, accessed July 7, 2021, https://adage.com/article/special-report-cannes-lions/geico-s-pre-roll-leica-s-100-ad-film-grand-prix-john-lewis-monty-wins-top-prize-film-craft/299257.

18 "Nonprofit Marketing Statistics: Preparing Your Strategy Through 2017," Ironpaper, accessed May 12, 2021, https://www.ironpaper.com/webintel/articles/nonprofit-marketing-statistics-2017/.

19 "Antoine de Saint-Exupéry Quotes," Brainy Quote, accessed June 21, 2021, https://www.brainyquote.com/quotes/antoine_de_saintexupery_121261.

20 "How Emotions Influence Purchasing Behaviour," Adcock Solutions, accessed June 21, 2021, https://www.adcocksolutions.com/post/how-emotions-influence-purchasing-behaviour.

21 "Building meaningful is good for business: 77% of consumers buy brands who share their values," Havas Media Group, accessed May 13, 2021, https://havasmedia.com/building-meaningful-is-good-for-business-77-of-consumers-buy-brands-who-share-their-values/.

22 Ibid.

23 Drucker, Peter F., *Managing the Non-profit Organization* (New York: Harper Collins, 1990), 56.

24 Siebert, Mark, "EST Training: In order to win, you've got to be bigger, faster, easier & cheaper," *Franchise Times,* accessed June 21, 2021, https://www.franchisetimes.com/article_archive/est-training/article_63d20bc7-7474-51e8-be46-bd33752ecc92.html.

25 Ibid.

26 "Go West, Young Man, Go West," Encyclopedia.com, accessed June 16, 2021, https://www.encyclopedia.com/history/dictionaries-thesauruses-pictures-and-press-releases/go-west-young-man-go-west.

27 Suby, Sabri, *Sell Like Crazy: How to Get As Many Clients, Customers and Sales As You Can Possibly Handle* (self-published, 2019).

28 Ibid.

29 Sherman, Lisa, "5 Ways to Find Inspirational News and Mobilize People During the Pandemic," The Ad Council, accessed May 5, 2021, https://www.adcouncil. org/all-articles/5-ways-marketers-can-mobilize-and-find-inspiration-during-the-pandemic.

30 "Nonprofit Taglines: The Art of Effective Brevity," *Nonprofit Quarterly,* accessed June 21, 2021, https://nonprofitquarterly.org/nonprofit-taglines-the-art-of-effective-brevity/.

31 Ibid.

32 "Larry Keeley," Institute of Design, accessed May 26, 2021, https://id.iit.edu/ people/larry-keeley/.

33 Sontag, Andy, "The 5E Experience Design Model," UX Blog, accessed May 26, 2021, https://medium.theuxblog.com/the-5e-experience-design-model-7852324d46c.

34 Ibid.

35 Jeffries, Isaac, "The 5 E's of Customer Journey," accessed May 26, 2021, https:// isaacjeffries.com/blog/2016/5/17/the-5-es-of-customer-journey..

36 Strom, Stephanie, "To Help Donors Choose, Web Site Alters How It Sizes Up Charities," The New York Times, accessed March 27, 2021, https://www.nytimes. com/2010/11/27/business/27charity.html.

37 Ibid.

38 Godin, Seth, *Purple Cow: Transform Your Business by Being Remarkable* (Penguin Books, 2007).

39 "Nonprofit Sector Growing Faster Than For-Profit," 501(c) Agencies Trust, accessed July 7, 2021, https://www.501ctrust.org/nonprofit-sector-growing-faster-than-for-profit/..

40 "By 2030, Each Person Will Own 15 Connected Devices—Here's What That Means for Your Business and Content," *MTA Martech Advisor,* accessed July 7, 2021, https://www.martechadvisor.com/articles/iot/by-2030-each-person-will-own-15-connected-devices-heres-what-that-means-for-your-business-and-content/.

41 McLuhan, Marshall, *Understanding Media: The Extensions of Man* (Signet Books, 1964), 9.

42 Bagin, Rich, APR, "Pat Jackson's Place on PR Mount Rushmore," Always Something, accessed June 23, 2021, https://schoolpr.wordpress.com/2016/09/12/pat-jacksons-place-on-prs-mount-rushmore/.

43 Butler, Hannah, "6 Steps to Get the Press to Tell Your Story," DO MORE GOOD,

accessed June 23, 2021, https://membership.domoregood.org/posts/steps-to-get-the-press-to-tell-your-story.

44 Brodwin, David, "How Companies Can Do Well While Doing Good," *U.S. News and World Report*, accessed June 18, 2021, https://www.usnews.com/opinion/blogs/economic-intelligence/2013/06/03/for-benefit-businesses-show-profits-and-good-deeds-go-hand-in-hand.

45 Drucker, Peter F., "What Business Can Learn from Nonprofits," *Harvard Business Review*, accessed June 18, 2021, https://hbr.org/1989/07/what-business-can-learn-from-nonprofits.

46 De Vos, Rich, *Compassionate Capitalism*, Dutton Books, https://www.publishersweekly.com/978-0-525-93567-4.

47 Mackey, John, *Conscious Capitalism: Liberating the Heroic Spirit of Business*, Harvard Business Review Press, 2013.

48 "Boosting the 'Fourth-sector' Economy is Goal of 200-delegate Summit at Harvard," 3BL CSRWire, accessed June 20, 2021, https://www.csrwire.com/press_releases/35643-boosting-the-fourth-sector-economy-is-goal-of-200-delegate-summit-at-harvard.

49 Vella, Melanie, "How to Go Beyond Brand Purpose and Unlock New Relationships with Consumers," *Sustainable Brands*, accessed June 18, 2021, https://sustainablebrands.com/read/marketing-and-comms/how-to-go-beyond-brand-purpose-and-unlock-new-relationships-with-consumers.

50 Ibid.

51 *Close Encounters of the Third Kind*, IMDB, accessed June 18, 2021, https://www.imdb.com/title/tt0075860/.

52 Campbell, Julia, *Storytelling in the Digital Age: A Guide for Nonprofits* (CharityChannel Press, 2017).

53 Latasha Doyle, "How Nonprofits Can Build Partnerships with Businesses," Candid, August 19, 2020, https://blog.candid.org/post/how-nonprofits-can-build-partnerships-with-businesses/.

54 From Four Hundred Texts on Love 1.31-32, "Sayings of Saint Maximus the Confessor," *Orthodox Christianity*, accessed August 14, 2021, https://orthochristian.com/100726.html.